OUR
READERS RAVE

Some books you read print fancy reviews written by fancy book critics. Borrring! At the BRI, we care more about what our faithful readers have to say.

"Since sharing my *Bathroom Reader* with my friends at school, my popularity has dramatically increased. Thanks!"

—Chance G., age 13

"Most of my friends don't read. They see movies. But to me the book is always better than the movie. If your books cost $50, I would buy them. They rock!"

—Rene C.

"On a scale of 1 to 10, I love ur books at about a...13.5."

—Zolly C., age 14

"I got the Kids edition for Christmas! I love it. I frequently find myself in a position where my brother is banging on the door screaming at me to get out of the bathroom...tee-hee, thanks! :)"

—Lindsay P., age 12

"When I discovered the *Bathroom Reader for Kids Only* at the airport, it changed my life. I would like to thank you...I'll never be bored again!!!!"

—Dominika D., age 11

"The minute I opened up the *Bathroom Reader for Kids Only*, I couldn't close it! I take it to school, and all my friends want to read it! Thanks, B.R.I."

—Toria Z., age 9

"Hey, everyone who helps out at the Bathroom Readers' Institute. I am a HUGE fan. I have over 20 Bathroom Readers, and I read them lots. You guys are awesome. Keep up the good work!"

—Your longtime leg-numbing loo-sitter reader, *Josiah P., age 14*

"I really love your *Bathroom Reader*, I read it everywhere. It's better than Harry Potter and definitely the best thing since sliced bread."

—Richard L., age 12

"I have 14-year-old twin boys…one reads everything, anything, and everything. The other won't read anything at all…except the Bathroom Readers."

—Jonna W.

"My best memory is the first time I ever saw a Bathroom Reader that I got for Christmas. I am VERY notorious for my 'reading habits,' and when my parents gave me that book that had those enchanting words *Bathroom Reader* on the cover, I was totally bowled over."

—Corey L.

"Just finished reading *For Kids Only*. (OK, I'm a 50-year-old kid, but my wife and mom said it was OK.)"

—Chris P.

Uncle John's
Totally Quacked

BATHROOM READER FOR KIDS ONLY!

By the Bathroom Readers' Institute

Bathroom Readers' Press
Ashland, Oregon

UNCLE JOHN'S BATHROOM TOTALLY QUACKED BATHROOM READER® FOR KIDS ONLY

For information, write:
Bathroom Readers' Institute
P.O. Box 1117, Ashland, OR 97520
www.bathroomreader.com

Cover design and illustration by Pete Whitehead
Interior Illustration by Luis Filella

ISBN-13: 978-1-62686-175-6 / ISBN-10: 1-62686-175-7

Library of Congress Cataloging-in-Publication Data

Uncle John's totally quacked bathroom reader for kids only!
    pages cm

ISBN 978-1-62686-175-6 (hard cover)

1. American wit and humor--Juvenile literature. 2. Wit and humor, Juvenile. 3. Curiosities and wonders--Juvenile literature. I. Title: Totally quacked bathroom reader for kids only! II. Title: For kids only.
    PN6166.U5855 2014
    818'.5402--dc23   2013047738

Printed in the United States of America
First Printing: 2014

19 18 17 16 15 14   6 5 4 3 2 1

THANK YOU!

*The Bathroom Readers' Institute thanks those people
whose help has made this book possible.*

Gordon Javna

Kim T. Griswell

Jay Newman

Brian Boone

Trina Janssen

Pete Whitehead

Luis Filella

Carly Schuna

Rich Wallace

Sandra Neil Wallace

Mark Haverstock

Nancy Coffelt

Molly Marcot

Megan Todd

Elizabeth Armstrong Hall

Tracy Vonder Brink

Vijaya Khisty Bodach

Hannah Halliday

Joan M. Kyzer

Blake Mitchum

Rusty von Dyl

Brandon Walker

Melinda Allman

JoAnn Padgett

Aaron Guzman

Mana Manzvi

Ginger Winters

Jennifer Magee

Peter Norton

Sydney Stanley

Matt Lighty

R. R. Donnelley

Publishers Group West

The One and Only Rob Lowry

The Amazing Felix

Thomas Crapper

Lola Mae Bingham

The Voice

There isn't enough space to list the names of the
thousands of kids who have written to the BRI, but
without you, this book would have been impossible.

TABLE OF
CONTENTS

Because the BRI understands your reading needs, we've
divided the contents by length as well as subject:
Short—A quick read
Medium—2 pages
Long—3 to 5 pages (that's not too long, is it?)

GREETINGS FROM UNCLE JOHN

Hello, Totally Quacked Readers!

About a year ago, a small group of BRI members sat around a round table. Why? Because you can't sit *around* a *square* table, can you? Just kidding. Actually, we sat around the round table to brainstorm topics for our next fact-filled Bathroom Reader FOR KIDS ONLY!

"What should we write about?" I asked.

"Ninjas!" shouted Old Jaybeard.

"Ninjas?" Brian the Boy Wonder rolled his eyes. "I am so-o-o over ninjas."

"Smelly things!" barked Felix. (Yes, well-read canines are welcome at BRI meetings.)

"That is so-o-o last year," said the Boy Wonder.

"Quacky things," whispered a voice from a dark corner of the room.

That got my attention. "Do you mean quacky as in *charlatans, dissemblers, fakes, impostors,* and *mountebanks?*" I asked.

"Quackier…like a dog that had thirteen golf balls surgically removed from its stomach, and bomb-sniffing rats, and gummy-boogers candy, and a wedding dress made of human hair, and—"

"Wait a minute!" I held up a hand. "Are you just making stuff up, or are these things for real?"

"For real!"

"That is totally quacked!"

"Yes," said the voice. "Yes it is."

The result of that brainstorming session is in your hands: *Uncle John's Totally Quacked Bathroom Reader FOR KIDS ONLY!* It's stuffed fuller than a duck-down pillow with quackiness—goofy grownups, off-the-wall science, history's biggest nutcases, extreme sports, odd quotes, bird-brained jokes, brain games, and…ducks! Lots and lots of ducks.

Here's a sampling of what's inside:

- *Cooking with Pooh* and other books with stinky titles (page 42);
- "Miss Cakehead"—the British dessert maker who spooned fake vomit on lemon cupcakes (pages 66–67);
- The human actors behind Darkwing Duck, Count Duckula, and Quackula! (pages 76–77);
- Lady Mary Montagu's smallpox parties (pages 82–85);
- "If God were a cucumber" and other quacky things Canadians say (page 93);
- How to make a bug-size swimming pool (page 102);
- Chinese kids who go to school in a cave (pages 114–115);
- Barbie VS. Mrs. Potato Head (page 221); and much, much more!

Best of all, no matter how *crazy, cuckoo, deranged,* or *insane* the stuff in this book seems, we did not make it up. Every fact is brain-crackingly real. From the BRI round table, have a happy quack attack, and don't forget to…

Go with the Flow!

—Uncle John and the BRI staff

P.S. Visit us on the Web at *www.bathroomreader.com*

WHEN I WAS A KID

These celebs just might be st-r-r-retching the truth.

"My proudest moment as a child was when I beat my uncle Pierre at Scrabble with the seven-letter word FARTING."
—**Tina Fey**

"When I was a kid, I had two friends. They were imaginary, and they would only play with each other."
—**Rita Rudner**

"I was the kid next door's imaginary friend."
—**Emo Philips**

"When I was a kid my parents moved a lot. But I always found them."
—**Rodney Dangerfield**

"As a child my family's menu consisted of two choices: take it or leave it."
—**Buddy Hackett**

"When I was a little kid, we had a sandbox. It was a quicksand box. I was an only child...eventually."
—**Steven Wright**

"I was so naive as a kid I used to sneak behind the barn and do nothing."
—**Johnny Carson**

"When I was a kid, if a guy got killed in a western movie, I always wondered who got his horse."
—**George Carlin**

"We used to play spin the bottle when I was a kid. A girl would spin the bottle and if it pointed to you when it stopped, the girl could either kiss you or give you a dime. By the time I was 14, I owned my own home."
—**Gene Perret**

Did you know? An earthworm has five pairs of hearts.

I ONLY HAVE EYES FOR YOU

And you thought potatoes were trivial.

• Potatoes have a bad rep as a fattening food. They're not. In fact, they're 80 percent water and 99.9 percent fat-free. But the butter, sour cream, and cheese people load on top of potatoes is fat-a-licious.

• A medium-size potato with the peel contains more potassium than a banana and almost half the daily vitamin C requirement. Nutritionists call the misunderstood tuber "nature's perfect food."

• A typical potato weighs around half a pound, but the largest potato ever harvested weighed…more than 18 pounds. (Most adults' heads weigh only about 10 pounds.)

• The average German eats almost 250 pounds of potatoes each year.

• During Ireland's Potato Famine (1845–1851), the leaves and roots of potatoes caught a blight that turned them into a "slimy, decaying, blackish mass of rottenness." Some people were so desperate for food they ate seaweed or grass.

• The part of the potato that we eat grows belowground, but potato leaves and stems poke out of the soil. No matter how hungry you get, don't eat them. They contain a compound called *solanine*, which is toxic to humans.

• In the eighteenth century, Russians decided they'd rather starve than eat the lowly potato. The monarchy ordered that peasants who refused to eat potatoes have their ears and noses cut off.

A SNAG RAM

What's "a snag ram"? It's a rearrangement of the letters in the word "anagrams." It's also a hint for solving the anagrams below.

I. A COLD MOD LAND

Hint: Old __ __ __ __ __ __ __ __ __

2. BARF THE MET

Hint: Bet __ __ __ __ __ __ __

3. A CODGER SUNK YOUR WIT

Hint: Get Your __ __ __ __ __ in a __ __ __

4. OH ROSY SHOULDER

Hint: Hold Your __ __ __ __ __ __

5. WET ELF POOCH

Hint: Flew __ __ __ __ __ __ __

6. HUNG SNOT PIECE

Hint: __ __ __ __ __ __ __ __ Sheep

7. ON BRAIN BRAN

Hint: Born __ __ a __ __ __ __

Answers on page 283.

... got its name from the Native American word for the food: *batata.*

WORLD'S WORST VIDEO GAMES

Do you want to play these? We sure don't.

The Amazing Virtual Sea-Monkeys (PlayStation, 2002)

Here's the thing: Even "real" Sea-Monkeys always looked more interesting in the ads. In the ads, Sea-Monkeys were a family of smiling pink flipper-footed creatures living in a castle under the sea. What came in the Sea-Monkeys packet? Tiny white brine shrimp eggs. When hatched in water they grew up to be, well, shrimp. In the video game the creatures swimming around look more like naked potbellied people with antennae than like shrimp. Maybe that's why the Game Boy version was cancelled before its release.

Pro Cycling Manager 2005 (PC, 2005)

Bicycling video games can be fun—hit the buttons fast to pedal the wheels and watch out for sharp turns so you don't take spills. Too bad that's not what *Pro Cycling Manager 2005* is about. Instead of letting the player race on a cycling team, it makes the player *coach* the cycling team. So instead of pedaling faster, you get to tell virtual bicyclists that they should pedal faster.

Euro Truck Simulator (PC, 2008)

The best car video games involve driving superfast to win races. This game? It's all about how to drive a big-rig truck...safely. Challenges involve picking up cargo, making sure your rearview mirrors are picking up the road behind, and keeping the truck's

Oprah Winfrey and Elvis Presley are distant cousins.

speed within the legal limit. However, it is—or so the box says—"the very first simulation game set in Europe," so players get to see famous European landmarks along the way.

Bronkie the Bronchiasaurus (Super Nintendo, 1995)

A kid dinosaur has to save the planet after a meteor crashes and fills the earth with thick, cough-inducing dust. Sound promising? Yes, but here's the weird part—Bronkie the dinosaur has to save the world—and himself—with only his asthma inhaler. Seriously? Yep. This educational game was meant to teach kids *with* asthma *about* asthma.

Sensible Train Spotting (Amiga, 1995)

"Train spotting" has long been a popular activity for bored people in the United Kingdom. Train spotters sit near a train station, wait for a train to pass, and then take note of what kind of train it was. That's it. And somebody made a video game of it. The player sits…and waits for a train to go by. Then, the player looks at the number on the train and crosses it off a list of train numbers at the bottom of the screen. (Still awake? Neither are we.)

Desert Bus (PC, 1995)

This game was produced as a joke by the comedy/magic team Penn and Teller. Good news: It's supposed to be dumb. Bad news: It's not just dumb, it's boring. The player drives a bus from Arizona to Nevada at no more than 45 miles per hour. Really bad news: There's almost no scenery on the screen and play happens in *real time.* That's right. It takes eight hours to play the game and it can't be paused. (What? No potty breaks?) Worse news of all: the patient player receives one point for hanging on till the end.

BRAWHK! QUIZ!

How much do you know about parrots? (Brawhk! Parrots.)
The answers are on page 283. (Brawhk! Answers!)

1. A defining characteristic of a parrot is…

   a) a straight beak.

   b) a curved beak.

   c) dancing beak to beak.

2. Can all parrots imitate human speech?

   a) Yes

   b) Only African grey parrots

   c) Only those held in captivity by talkative humans

3. How many different kinds of parrots are there?

   a) Around 100

   b) 370…and counting

   c) They refuse to stand still and be counted.

4. Parrots are *zygodactyls*. What does that mean?

   a) They are a kind of flying dinosaur.

   b) They're pigeon-toed.

   c) Two of their toes point forward; two point backward.

5. Where are parrots *not* a native species?

   a) North America

   b) South America

   c) Africa

Got the blues? Bananas contain a natural chemical that makes you happy.

6. Polly may want a cracker, but which food will parrots refuse?

a) Seeds

(b) Meat

c) Fruit

7. Which parrot type is the most popular pet bird in the world?

a) Green-cheek conure

b) Blue macaw

(c) Budgie

8. Parrot eggs are always what color?

a) White

b) Light blue

(c) Yellow

9. How big are the biggest parrots?

a) A foot tall, weighing two pounds

b) About two feet tall, weighing three to four pounds

(c) About three feet tall, weighing as much as five pounds

10. What's a parrot's maximum lifespan?

a) As long as 60 years…on a pirate ship

(b) As long as 80 years…in the wild

c) As long as 25 years…caged at Grandma's house

Did you know? The first computer mouse (1963) was made of wood!

DOGS WILL BE DOGS

Think a dig through the kitchen trash is the worst your dog can do? Read on!

HOLE IN...13

A black Lab named Oscar spent a lot of time on the golf course in Fife, Scotland. He wasn't playing a few rounds. He was retrieving stray balls to bring home. That seemed harmless enough to his owner, Chris Morrison, until he noticed a rattling noise coming from Oscar as he walked around the house. Chris felt along Oscar's belly looking for the source of the noise. He found it: hard round objects that moved when he touched them. A trip to the vet and an hour-long operation later, 13 golf balls had been removed from the Lab's stomach. "It was like a magic trick," said the vet. "I opened him up and felt what I thought was two or three golf balls. But they just kept coming until we had a bag full." Turns out, Oscar isn't the only dog to snack on golf balls. Hannah, a yellow Lab from New Jersey racked up nine balls in the belly, and Zac, a Doberman from England, gobbled down five.

ONE-CLICK SHOPPING

In 2009, Greg Strope of Richmond, Virginia, received an e-mail confirming a $62 purchase of 5,000 Microsoft points. The points could be used to "buy" Xbox game content. One problem: Strope had not purchased $62 worth of Microsoft points. So who did? Strope had saved his credit card information in the system to make it easy to buy more points. That meant the purchase could have been made by anyone who had access to his system. Fortunately, the secret shopper left evidence—a slobbery chewed-up Xbox controller. Unfortunately, the Microsoft points Strope's dog managed to buy while chewing on the controller were nonrefundable.

COOL BEANS!

On a cold November evening in 2008, musician Bryan Maher parked his van and headed into the Cool Beanz coffee shop in Long Island, New York, to sign up for open-mic night. He left his car running with the heat on so his boxer, Bentley, wouldn't get a chill. Bentley jumped onto the driver's seat, moved the gear shift out of park, and started the van rolling. It rolled slowly—and surely—right into the coffee shop. The damage? A few pieces of broken patio furniture, a cracked store window, and minor dents and scratches to the van.

...is its drummer. His name? Frank Beard!

QUACKY CANDIES

Everybody likes a yummy piece of candy—but you might want to think twice about these.

BRAIN POPS

Sticking a sour-apple-flavored candy brain in your mouth might not seem all that disgusting. But once your tongue gets a lick of the lifelike brain-matter ridges covering the pop, your gag reflex might kick in. On the bright side, a fistful of Brain Pops makes the perfect bouquet for your favorite brain surgeon. ($2.95)

BOX OF BOOGERS

Looking for a treat guaranteed to gross out your friends? Pick these inch-long gummy snot nuggets. They come in three tasty flavors: Snottermelon, Sour Green Boogy, and Lemon Loogy. You can stick them to your fingertips and nostrils, and—best of all—when you roll them between your fingers, they feel just like the real deal! ($2.00 per box)

GUMMY HEART

Think you have a big heart? The average human heart weighs between 9 and 11 ounces, while this bright red gelatinous gummy heart weighs in at a heart-attack-inducing 16 ounces. That's a solid pound of gummy grossness—or goodness—if you keep in mind that it's cherry flavored and gluten free! ($15.00)

One out of four people in the world live on $1 per day.

ZOMBIE BLOOD

Real IV bags hang from stands beside hospital patients' beds. They drip fluids through a tube attached to a hollow needle stuck into a patient's vein (Ouch!). They're also used for blood transfusions, which is where the Zombie Blood Energy Potion comes in. We've heard the slime-green liquid contains the daily allowance of nutrients that the walking dead need to stay shuffling. But the label lists the same ingredients found in energy drinks for humans: 80 milligrams of caffeine plus iron, protein, and electrolytes. That's enough caffeine to keep you on the br-r-rains! hunt all night long. ($5.00)

ZIT POPPERS

If you need a gift for an older brother or sister, we have just the thing: a boxful of oozy, sticky, gummy zits. Squeeze the candy zits, and watermelon or strawberry gel spurts out (Yum!). ($1.99)

HOSE NOSE

Looking for a nose-shaped candy dispenser you can strap to your face and slide over your real nose? We thought so. This one oozes sour-apple slime from its nostrils. Just squeeze the plastic schnoz, stick out your tongue, and catch the drips. ($2.95)

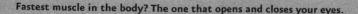

Fastest muscle in the body? The one that opens and closes your eyes.

PRESIDENTIAL POTTIES

With 35 of them scattered over six residential levels, it's no wonder weird things have happened in White House bathrooms.

TUB TROUBLE

In 1824, President James Monroe invited the Marquis de Lafayette to the U.S. to celebrate the fiftieth anniversary of the American Revolution. The French nobleman had fought in America's war for independence and become a war hero. Lafayette spent a year touring all 24 states (that's all there were back then). By the time he finally showed up at the White House, Monroe was no longer in office. President John Quincy Adams welcomed the marquis into what was now his home, but the president's wife, First Lady Louisa Catherine Adams was not pleased. Why? Because Lafayette had picked up a lot of swag along the way. He brought a ton of luggage with him and...a live alligator. The gator lived in the bathtub of the East Room of the White House for months.

PLUMB CRAZY

White House plumber Howard "Reds" Arrington fixed the toilets of every president from Harry S. Truman to Jimmy Carter. During the Truman administration he got a frantic call: the First Lady's toilet wasn't flushing correctly. Reds rushed right over and found the problem: a pair of false teeth clogging the works. "They weren't Mrs. Truman's," Reds told reporters. "They were her maid's."

Liechtenstein (the 6th smallest country) exports the most false teeth.

AN UNINVITED GUEST

During a World War II-era visit to President Roosevelt, British prime minister Winston Churchill decided to have a relaxing soak in the tub at the end of a long day. After his bath, Churchill strolled naked and dripping into his connecting bedroom only to discover the president standing in front of the fireplace. The good news? It wasn't President Roosevelt. The bad news? It was President Lincoln—who'd been dead for more than 75 years. Legend has it Churchill said, "Good evening, Mr. President. You seem to have me at a disadvantage."

SHOWER POWER

One morning in 1969, White House chief of staff Bob Haldeman walked into the Oval Office. He had a stack of papers for President Richard M. Nixon to sign. The president was too busy. He was pouring over plumbing catalogs trying to find a new showerhead for his shower. It seems the previous president—Lyndon Baines Johnson—had installed a showerhead so powerful that when Nixon used it, the water blew him against the wall and nearly knocked him off his feet.

STARSTRUCK

In 2013, President Barack Obama invited Damian Lewis, star of TV's *Homeland* series, to a state dinner. Other guests included actor George Clooney and British prime minister David Cameron. But the *Homeland* star wasn't as starstruck by the VIPs as he was by the White House itself. "We took snaps of each other in every room," his wife told reporters. "Including the loo. Thrilling!" (*Snaps* is short for snapshots and *loo*? That's British slang for…bathroom.)

Favorite word of actor Mark Hamill (Luke Skywalker)? *Pixilated!*

HERE COMES TROUBLE

Nelson Mandela (1918–2013) spent 27 years in a South African prison for fighting against an unfair system. And then...he was elected president. His birth name, Rolihlahla means "troublemaker." Here are some quotes by, and about, the man.

"A winner is a dreamer who never gives up."

"I cannot fully imagine my own life without the example Nelson Mandela set."
—President Barack Obama

"No one is born hating another person because of the color of his skin, or his background, or his religion. People must learn to hate, and if they can learn to hate, they can be taught to love, for love comes more naturally to the human heart."

"Lead from the back—and let others believe they are in front."

"Mandela and I never met because of my schedule and because of him not knowing who I was. We respected each other that way."
—Stephen Colbert,
The Colbert Report

"Courage is not the absence of fear—it's inspiring others to move beyond it."

"Do not judge me by my successes, judge me by how many times I fell down and got back up again."

"Don't call me. I'll call you."
—Nelson Mandela,
when he left office on his
86th birthday

SLICE OF PI

If you have an image of a yummy, crusty, apple-filled dessert in your mind right now, think again. Pi isn't pie. Pi is the ratio of a circle's circumference to its diameter. Usually written as 3.14159, it's a number only a math geek could truly love.

Believe it or not, March 14 is a holiday: Pi Day. The U.S. Congress passed a resolution to make it official in 2009. You can't "officially" skip school on that day, but if you do, you could join in a bunch of cool math-geek celebrations.

Princeton University throws one of the biggest bashes. In the past, its Pi Day celebrations have lasted almost a full week. Along with a contest to see who can recite the most digits of pi (computers have calculated pi to over 10 trillion [10^{13}] digits), the university holds a pie-eating competition, a pie-making competition, and a pie-throwing competition, where participants can lob a cream pie at a frenemy of their choice.

At the San Francisco Exploratorium, math lovers who arrive for the festivities are handed a pie plate attached to a numbered yardstick. They arrange themselves in order of pi's digits and march 3.14 times around a "pi shrine" while singing "Happy Birthday" to Albert Einstein, whose birthday happens to be on Pi Day.

If you really want to kick your pi partying up a notch, you can try besting Theresa Miller's way of celebrating—but good luck! The University of New Mexico student started her own Pi Day tradition in 2008. It involves hula-hooping, solving a Rubik's Cube, and reciting pi to 450 digits all at the same time. Eat that, math haters!

Cucumbers are the only food a cockroach won't eat.

ANIMAL ESCAPES

No zoo could permanently hold these daring creatures.

- A two-year-old sea lion named Zola had lived at Karlsruhe Zoo in Germany since birth. In August 2013, she left her enclosure… but not for freedom. She left to join the swans in the pond next door. A zoo official said Zola was either "curious" or "wanted some time away from her parents." The young sea lion stayed with the swans for over a month and then made her way back home to Mom and Dad.

- In 1987 a Japanese macaque (a fuzzy pink-faced primate) named Alphie decided he didn't want to live in the monkey house of the Pittsburgh Zoo anymore. So he left. Numerous people spotted Alphie in the Pittsburgh area and throughout Pennsylvania, but he couldn't be caught. Finally, six months later, the macaque was tracked down. Where was he? In Ohio, more than 100 miles away from the Pittsburgh Zoo. He was quickly returned to his monkey-house home.

- Q: How did 15 camels, a few llamas, and a pig break out of the circus? A: The giraffe planned the whole thing. It happened in the Amsterdam suburb of Amstelveen in the Netherlands in 2008. Just before dawn, the giraffe kicked open a fence— officials say he was the only one of the animals strong enough to have done that kind of damage. When the giraffe walked out, the camels, llamas, and a potbellied pig followed. Troupe members rounded up the escapees (it's pretty easy to spot a giraffe in a suburban neighborhood) before they could make much mischief.

There is more bacteria in your mouth than there are people on Earth.

- In March 2012, the Tokyo Sea Life Park received an e-mailed picture from a concerned citizen. Could the Humboldt penguin photographed playing in nearby Tokyo Bay be one of the zoo's penguins? After a head count, park officials discovered that they were, in fact, one penguin short. To escape into Tokyo Bay, the missing penguin, just a year old and unable to fly, would have had to scale a wall twice its height. Tokyo Sea Life Park officials told citizens to leave capturing the penguin to professionals. It took the pros two months to catch the penguin napping and bring it home.

- What led an orangutan named Karta to break out of her area in Australia's Adelaide Zoo in 2009? Probably boredom. "She's always trying to outsmart the keepers, and today she showed a touch of genius," said zoo curator Peter Whitehead. Karta broke free by twisting a stick around some of the electrified wires circling her enclosure until the fence short-circuited. With the fence off, she made a pile of shrubs and branches, climbed on top of it, and scaled the fence. When she saw keepers standing by with tranquilizer guns ready to foil her escape, Karta was smart enough to jump back inside.

WHO ORDERED FRIES?

Solve this fast-food puzzle.

The Beagle brothers got a bag of food from the take-out window at Lefty's Burgers. They drove to a picnic table in the park to chow down, but when they opened the bag, they discovered a problem. Each brother thought he ordered fries, but there were only three containers of fries in the bag.

> Biddy is five years older than Diddy.
>
> Kiddy is two years younger than Biddy.
>
> Piddy is three years older than Diddy.

"The three older brothers should get the fries," said Piddy.

"No," said Diddy, "the three younger ones should."

"Just make sure we don't get pickles!" said the twins in unison. "We're allergic to them."

"I know I ordered fries," said the oldest brother, "because I didn't order dessert."

"Check the receipt," said Kiddy. "That will show us who forgot to order fries. That's who won't get any."

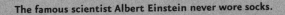

The famous scientist Albert Einstein never wore socks.

Here's the receipt that shows the four orders.

Order 1

Lefty Burger, no pickles
Fries
Apple pie
Root beer

Order 2

Lefty Burger, loaded
Fries
Grape soda

Order 3

Lefty burger, extra cheese
Ice-cream sandwich
Cola

Order 4

Lefty Burger, no pickles
Fries
Giant cookie
Orange soda

So, who forgot to order fries?

Answer on page 283.

First fruit eaten on the Moon? A peach.

ASK THE EXPERTS

There will always be more questions than answers, but here are a couple you can stop scratching your head about.

YOU'RE MY TYPE

Q: *How can you tell a girl earthworm from a boy earthworm?*

A: You can't! Earthworms, like snails, are hermaphrodites. That means that each earthworm is both male and female! Each worm can produce both eggs and sperm to fertilize the eggs. This helps worms considerably, since their burrowing prevents them from meeting often. (*Backyard Pets: Activities for Exploring Wildlife Close to Home* by Carol A. Amato)

SEEING THE LIGHT

Q: *How do worms see in the dark underground?*

A: They don't, because worms have no eyes. They simply move slowly and feel their way around. Despite their lack of eyes, they do sense the light, because they have light-sensitive organs on their heads and tails. Why do they care about light if they can't see? Sunlight would dry out their skin and eventually kill them, so that's why they live underground. (*How Much Does Your Head Weigh? The Big Fat Book of Facts* by Marg Meikle)

Google, Hewlett Packard, Microsoft, and Apple were all started in garages.

TWO WORMS ARE DEADER

Q: *If I cut an earthworm in half will it grow into two worms?*
A: No. If you cut an earthworm in half, all you will usually end up with is two halves of a dead worm. Like most creatures, an earthworm cut in half will probably die. The only way it might survive is if the cut is made behind the thickest part of the worm, which is called the saddle, where all its major organs are found. If all these organs are retained, the worm may survive, since it should be able to regenerate a new anus. But if a cut is made anywhere in front of the saddle, the earthworm is certain to die. (*Why Dogs Eat Poop, and other Useless or Gross Information about the Animal Kingdom* by Francesca Gould and David Haviland)

FOOD FOR WORMS

Q: *What do worms eat?*
A: Worms eat by swallowing bits of food matter and digesting it in a crop and gizzard system. Like chickens, they swallow tiny stones they then store in their gizzard to use as millstones. Worms don't just swallow nutritious stuff; like many a kid, they eat dirt. In fact, Aristotle called them "the intestines of the earth," suggesting they went about digesting the planet. And they do. Worms pass enough dirt through their bodies to cover an average acre with two-tenths of an inch of "castings" a year. You can see these castings scattered around worm burrows, and some species use them to build towers and hills. Like human waste, worm casts add up: an acre of dirt two-tenths of an inch thick is eighteen tons of worm waste a year. But we're lucky: In South Africa, the stuff piles up so fast farmers use bulldozers to scrape it away. (*Aliens in the Backyard: Plant and Animal Imports into America* by John Leland)

RAINY DAY PLAY

Q: *Why are there worms all over the sidewalk after it rains?*

A: A common worm myth is that when it rains worms come out of their burrows to keep from drowning. Well, there are several possible reasons for this behavior—and none of them deal with drowning. One reason is that worms come out of their burrows when it rains so they can find a mate. Another one is that CO_2 levels in the burrow build up due to respiration, forming a weak acid solution that worms do not like. Whatever the reason, studies have shown that worms can remain alive in aerated water. Fish breeders who feed worms to their fish report that worms can live for many months under the filter trays in aquariums. A bigger danger to worms is drying out. (*The Worm Book* by Loren Nancarrow and Janet Hogan Taylor)

RANDOM WORM FACTS

- An earthworm's favorite treat to eat? Other earthworms!

- In Norway, scientists studied whether earthworms felt pain. They don't. (Or if they do, they're not telling.)

- There are around 4,400 different types of earthworms.

- Worm species are still being discovered. A new one (indigo blue with yellow spots) was found in the Philippines in 2001.

- Ribbon worms are the world's longest animal. In the 1860s, an 180-foot-long specimen was found in Scotland. What do they eat? Dead or dying animals.

WEATHER OR NOT

Outfit your pooch for all kinds of weather.

THE WEATHER: Chilly
THE GEAR: Sherpa Dog Boots. With fake suede on the outside, fluffy fabric on the inside, and grooved rubber soles, these toasty boots will keep your pooch's paws warm. They come in six sizes and three colors, but it's up to you to convince your dog to be still and give you his feet. ($23.99)

THE WEATHER: Flood
THE GEAR: K-9 Float Coat™. Designed to help dogs swim and stay afloat, this vest-like coat has foam panels, reflective borders, and even a handle for lifting your dog out of the water. ($79.95)

THE WEATHER: Spring rain
THE GEAR: PawZ dog boots. Made of natural rubber, these brightly colored pull-on socks do for your dog what galoshes do for you: let you splash in puddles without getting your feet wet. They're disposable, 100% biodegradable, work well for avoiding fire ants' stings, too! ($15.95, 12-pack)

THE WEATHER: Sunny
THE GEAR: Designer-Dogwear Sunsuit. Don't let the sun fry your dog, especially if he has short fur or pale skin. Cover him up with a spandex-type bodysuit designed to block the sun's harmful UV radiation. Suits look something like a surfer's wetsuit and come with handy cutouts for male or female dogs. Vets recommend sunsuits with 50 SPF or higher. ($39.95)

EWW...FOOD

Think fast food makes a quick and tasty meal?
These people got more than they ordered.

ORGAN-ICK FOOD

A couple from Ocala, Florida, decided to stop at their local
Popeyes for a snack to take home to their kid. Inside the box they
found a little something extra dangling from the chicken breast
they'd ordered: a dark, shriveled chicken heart—or maybe a liver.
Seems it's hard to tell one deep-fried chicken organ from another.

SELF-SLICING SANDWICH

A 27-year-old New Yorker got more than he ordered in his Subway
sandwich. When he bit into the bread, his teeth hit metal. What
was it? According to the sandwich snacker, a 7-inch knife had been
baked into the bread.

FRY FIRST AID

While a senior at the University of Illinois, Lauren Coleman bought
fries from McDonald's at the student union food court. She found
more in her fry bag than she paid for: a used Band-Aid. Though
she received an apology from the manager and a brand new meal,
she's now a bit skeptical about fast food. "It's a lesson for me and
everyone on campus," Coleman said. "Look in your bag before you
leave. There could be someone's dentures or hair inside there." On
the positive side, the fry cook came out and apologized in person.
"I'm sorry," she said. "That's my Band-Aid."

It is illegal to wiggle while dancing in California.

TRIPLE THREAT

Army staff sergeant Clark Bartholomew ordered a Burger King Triple Stacker from the Schofield Barracks Burger King in Hawaii and took it home to chow down. That's when he bit into something sharp that made his tongue bleed. What he found in his burger? A needle. But it gets worse. Another needle made its way into Bartholomew's small intestine and he had to be hospitalized for six days.

SKINWICH

David Scheiding ordered a chicken sandwich at an Arby's in Tipp City, Ohio. When he took a bite, the lettuce didn't seem as fresh and crisp as he'd hoped. Turns out, some of the lettuce wasn't lettuce at all. On top of the sandwich, Scheiding found a piece of flesh about three-fourths of an inch long. When health investigators came to question the restaurant manager, he was wearing a latex glove. Beneath the glove? A bandage on his thumb. The manager admitted he had sliced skin from his thumb while shredding lettuce. He had sanitized the area but didn't throw away the bin of lettuce with the shredded skin in it.

SNOT A CONDIMENT

Deputy Sheriff Edward Bylsma stopped for lunch at a Burger King in Vancouver, Washington. He ordered a Whopper. When he peeled back the bun to make sure everything was okay, he saw a huge white glob sitting on top of the patty. Bylsma didn't eat the burger. He sent it to the lab. DNA testing identified the glob (it was spit) and the culprit: Burger King employee Gary Herb. Herb pleaded guilty to assault and was sentenced to 90 days in jail.

In the original Cinderella, the slipper was made of fur (not glass).

QUACKED QUOTES

Uncle John's Totally Quacked Bathroom Reader *wouldn't be complete without a few words from Disney's* DuckTales *animated TV series.*

Viking I: "Feeding the prisoners to the sharks isn't any fun."
Viking 2: "It is for the sharks!"

Scrooge McDuck: "If Duckburg studios is going to survive, Major Courage is going to need a major overhaul."
Major Courage: "Uh... How major?"
Scrooge: "Major major, Major."

"C'mon, even E.T. got to phone home."
—Launchpad McQuack

Huey: "Hey, why would a ghost need to use a door?"
Dewey: "Is that a riddle or a knock-knock joke?"

"Somebody stop those pants!"
—Scrooge McDuck

Scrooge McDuck: "Banana Island is probably full of pearls."
Duckworth: "Or bananas."

"We don't need facts. We're in television!"
—Laurence Loudmouth

"Efficiency has its place, but not in my hot chocolate."
—Scrooge McDuck

Launchpad McQuack: "Say, why don't we find ourselves some spoons and dig our way out of here."
Scrooge McDuck: "Launchpad, how did you ever manage to survive childhood?"

"Duckworth, go off and make big butts...I mean big bucks!"
—Scrooge McDuck

Christopher Columbus brought the first orange seeds to the New World in 1493.

FACE TIME

What happens if you shut down your computer? You can have real-time fun playing Face Time with friends or family.

WHAT YOU NEED

- a blank 4 x 5 bingo card for each player
- a pencil with eraser for each player
- small crackers, such as Goldfish or Oyster Crackers

F	A	C	E
Uncle John	Cat	Peru	Ice Cream

WHAT TO DO

1. Have players write the letters **F-A-C-E** across the top row of their cards.

2. Next, have them fill in the empty boxes with words that correspond to these four categories: **F**amous people, **A**nimals, **C**ountries, and **E**ats (**F-A-C-E**).

HOW TO PLAY

1. After the boxes are filled, the game begins. Each player takes a turn being caller. The caller makes up a phrase that corresponds to one of the FACE categories. For example: "A Famous writer." If you wrote down Uncle John or another writer in the Famous person category, place a cracker in that bingo square. **Note:** *The caller does not mark his or her card, and players can mark only one square per call.*

2. The first person to successfully complete a **F-A-C-E** row or column wins! And then…players get to eat their crackers, erase their boards, and start again.

If you lift its tail off the ground, a kangaroo can't hop.

PARROT REPORT

The world's smartest birds...in the news.

FORMERLY A PARROT

In 2005, Itzik Simkowitz of Beersheba, Israel, bought a cockatoo at a pet shop for the equivalent of $2,000. But when Simkowitz got his new pet bird home, he noticed something very strange—the cockatoo wasn't alive. (It had died somewhere between the store and Simkowitz's home.) The pet shop owner insisted that the cockatoo was just sleepy and was shy over having to adjust to a new home. He refused to return Simkowitz's money.

DIRTY BIRD

The Humane Society of Charlotte, North Carolina, offers up a wide variety of pets for adoption, from dogs and cats to the more exotic, such as African grey parrots. In 2004, however, it had to abruptly remove a parrot from the adoption list. The problem? African greys are very good at mimicking human speech and sounds. It seems the parrot had picked up (or been taught) some questionable things by its former owner: vulgar words...and fart sounds.

JAIL? BIRD

In August 2013, a 21-year-old parakeet in Tampa, Florida, named Emerald began squawking a lot louder than usual (parakeets don't talk). That got the attention of her owner, Suzette Beesley—which is exactly what Emerald had wanted. Beesley looked out the window next to Emerald's cage and saw what Emerald was

Average lifespan of a Major League baseball? Seven pitches.

squawking about: somebody was trying to break into the neighbor's house. Beesley called 9-1-1 as Emerald kept squawking and staring out the window. Police arrived and arrested the suspect. "We pretty much don't have a watchdog," Beesley said, "but we have a watch*bird* for the neighborhood."

YELLOW-BILLED YAPSTER

In 2013 visitors to the waiting room of a veterinarian's office in Belgrade, Serbia, were startled by the sound of a yapping dog. What's so odd about that? The sounds were coming from the vet's pet parrot. Apparently, after listening day after day to all that doggy whining, the parrot—whose cage was in the waiting room—decided to join in.

NEW CREW

When a crew started construction on a new community center near Michelle Cassie's home in Newmachar, England, she wasn't prepared for the noise. Beeping lorries (that's British for construction trucks), giant drills, and heavy-duty grinders turned her peaceful neighborhood into noise central. But that wasn't the worst part. What was? Cassie's pet parrot, Simba, started mimicking the building-site sounds. "The parrot is just copying anything," said Cassie. "She makes grinding noises, truck noises, and the beeping noise the cherry picker makes when it's reversing." The day-to-day sounds of construction are bad enough, Cassie says, but what if Simba keeps mimicking the sounds after construction ends? "We just hope she stops when it's finished."

A manatee eats between 100 to 150 pounds of plants daily!

COOKING WITH POOH

What were these authors thinking? We have no idea! But we couldn't resist sharing these book titles and descriptors.

What's Your Poo Telling You? by Anish Sheth, M.D. and Josh Richman. Need to know the difference between a "floater" and a "hanging chad"? This book gives you the inside poop, uh...scoop.

Everybody Poops 410 Pounds a Year: An Illustrated Bathroom Companion for Grown-Ups by Deuce Flanagan. Fascinating facts about that thing everyone does but no one wants to talk about (except, apparently, this guy).

The Truth About Poop by Susan E. Goodman. "Birds drop it as bombs. Sharks track their prey with it. People use it as a Frisbee."

The Long Journey of Mr. Poop/El gran viaje del Señor Caca by Angèle Delaunois. Who could resist a bilingual story starring a wolf in a lab coat who explains why the large intestine doesn't exactly smell like roses.

Poop Happened! A History of the World from the Bottom Up by Sarah Albee. "This book takes readers inside the fascinating world of excrement." (Wow!)

Cooking with Pooh by Mouse Works. Okay. We confess. This one's not about poop with a "p." Winnie-the-Pooh and pals Eeyore, Tigger, and Roo share recipes for cookies and sandwiches and pizza.

HAIR TO SPARE

In today's fashion industry, Rapunzel would have made it big!

HERE COMES THE BRIDE, ALL DRESSED IN...HAIR?

Hairdresser Ryan Edwards of Liverpool, England, collected enough hair from his salon to make 10,000 hair wefts (a "weft" is a long strip of hair that's used in hair extensions). Those hair wefts were then used by designer Thelma Madine to create a multicolored wedding dress weighing 33 pounds. A team of eight people spent 300 hours making the dress, and Madine put a price tag of 50,000 British pounds (around $77,000 U.S.) on her creation. "I'd be overwhelmed if someone like Lady Gaga would consider wearing it," says Madine. "It's a unique creation, just like her, and I think it would be a hair match made in heaven!"

A KILLER SUIT

An "apex predator" is a predator that's at the very top of the food chain—like bald eagles, tigers, orcas, and crocodiles. The Apex Predator Suit was designed for the ultimate predator: humans. The creative team behind the Apex line—Fantich & Young—aren't just making clothes. They're making an artistic statement. Their work, so they claim, looks at the "parallels between social evolution and evolution in the natural world." The suit is completely covered in human hair. It has glass eyes and small bones where most suits have buttons. And there are shoes to match, with teeth (1,050 of them) forming the tread on the soles. Relax, they're not real teeth. They're teeth from dentures. Wear if you dare!

... to return the baseball he hit for his 700th career home run.

IT'S "CHEST" A COAT

When Wing-Co, a drink company, wanted to promote their manly new chocolate-flavored protein drink, they did more than buy ad space. They had four designers spend more than 200 hours making a coat entirely out of one million strands of…men's chest hair (Ouch!). Three hundred men donated chest hair for the Man-Fur Coat—enough fluff to fill more than a dozen cardboard boxes. The coat, priced at almost $4,000 was meant to send a message to British men. Says a spokesperson from Wing-Co: "Whether it's their appetite or their appearance, men all over the U.K. need to man-up."

HAIR'S TO THE FUTURE

Charlie Le Mindu is the designer behind Lady Gaga's, uhm…*hairy couture*, including those human-hair dresses she sometimes wears. Le Mindu's creations sell for as much as $30,000. They range from hats to whole suits, but they share one thing in common: They're all made from hair.

According to Le Mindu, Lady Gaga isn't the only one wearing human hair. But she *is* one of the few who does it on purpose. Plenty of others wear human hair without knowing it. That's because some less-than-honest fur-coat makers thicken animal fur with less expensive human hair. Where is all this hair coming from? Most human hair comes from China and India. But anyone with long hair can cash in.

If the idea of wearing hair clothes freaks you out, you'd better get over it. "In ten years, we'll all be wearing clothes made from human hair," Le Mindu claims. The upside to hair clothes? "You can curl them or crimp them, and clean them with weekly brushing and dry shampoo."

Tee-hee-hee! **When a hyena "laughs" it's saying that it has food to share.**

MAKE IT GLOW!

*It's science; it's art; it's a really weird (but fun)
thing to do with a highlighter pen.*

WHAT YOU NEED

- a *nontoxic* yellow highlighter pen
- tap water
- clean quart jar with lid
- a black light (found in home improvement stores)

WHAT TO DO

1. Pop the end off the highlighter pen and pull out the ink-soaked felt interior. If you can't get it out, ask an adult for help.
2. Fill the jar with water. Place the inky felt inside and let the ink soak into the water.
3. Wait till after dark or find a dark closet (the darker, the better). Shine the black light on the water and watch it glow.
4. Seal the jar and store your glow-in-the-dark water. You can reuse it, and it will never fade.

HOW IT WORKS

The highlighter pen contains chemicals which are "phosphors." Phosphors absorb light and release it back. The light they're absorbing isn't visible light—it's ultraviolet light. Humans can only see colors in a spectrum ranging from red through orange, yellow, green, blue, and violet—ultraviolet is out of our range. We can see the purple glow a black light produces. But we can't see the

Mmmmm, fore! Honey is used to fill the center of golf balls.

ultraviolet ray the black light is also producing. Phosphors—like those in your glowing water—convert the UV light from the black light into a weird glowing light you can see.

GET YOUR GLOW ON

Don't just watch your jar of water glow. Make other things glow, too!

Glowing chalk: Soak sidewalk chalk in glowing water for several days. Let it dry. Draw on dark construction paper and let it glow.

Glowing flowers: Place cut flowers in a glass of glowing water. In a few hours the flowers will soak up enough of the phosphors that they'll glow in black light, too.

Glowing night-light: Take a clean empty jar, and paint designs on the outside with craft paint. Fill the jar with glow water, and put the lid back on. Use the black light to make your artsy night-light glow.

UNCLE JOHN SAYS doing science experiments like this one will make you smarter. But if you're already a genius (or too lazy to make glowing water), we have good news. Ordinary tonic water glows, too. It contains quinine, which is phosphorescent.

If you *really* want to have some fun, try this experiment. Take a liter of room-temperature tonic water and a roll of Mentos candies outside after dark. (Keep that black light handy. You're going to need it!) Find a piece of thin cardboard that can be rolled into a tube slightly bigger than the Mentos. Unwrap the candies and stack them inside the tube. (Keep a finger on the bottom so they don't drop out.) Turn on the black light. Line up the tube of Mentos exactly above the open mouth of the tonic-water bottle. Remove your finger and let the candies fall directly into the water.

Voilà! A shooting, glowing tonic-water fountain.

Alligators sometimes freeze on the surface of a pond for days...

WHY WE HAVE OCEANS

Christopher Columbus landed on the Bahamian island of San Salvador on October 12, 1492. He was greeted by natives, who welcomed him with the word "Taino." That means "good and noble people" in the native language, and also "peace." Columbus decided to call them the Taino people. This Taino myth tells why we have oceans—like the Atlantic Ocean that Columbus had just sailed across from Spain.

Yaya was a powerful god—the "spirit of the spirit." He had a son named Yayael, which means "son of Yaya."

As Yayael grew up, he became disobedient. He wanted to take over his father's kingdom. So his father sent him away for four months. The banishment did not work. When Yayael returned, he tried to kill his father. But Yaya would not give up his power. Instead, he killed his son.

Yaya loved his son and he regretted killing him. To keep Yayael nearby, Yaya put his son's bones in a hollow gourd and hung it from the ceiling of his hut.

One day Yaya looked into the gourd and was surprised to see that the bones had turned into water. Beautiful fish were swimming in it. Yaya ate some of the fish. The next day, many more fish had replaced them.

Each day, Yaya took fish from the gourd for his meal. A curious young boy named Deminan noticed what Yaya did. He waited until Yaya was away in the fields, and he sneaked over to see the gourd.

Deminan was amazed to see all the fish. He watched them for a long time, and he called his three brothers to eat some.

Then Deminan heard Yaya coming, and he hurried to return the gourd to its proper place. But he tripped, and the gourd fell to the ground. It broke into many pieces, and the water and the fish spilled out.

The water kept coming. It made streams and lakes, and it quickly overran the banks. Soon it had formed great oceans, teeming with fish.

And that is why we have oceans. They came from the bones of Yayael.

MLB umpires have to wear black underwear. Why? In case their pants split!

TONGUE TANGLERS

Tackle these tongue twisters thrice to test your talent!

Little ladybugs live under lily pads.

**Mustard mixed with mayonnaise makes
a sandwich wish it wasn't.**

Quick! A quack, a quail attack; attack a quail and, quick, quack!

Dairy-delivering dads deliver dairy to dozy domiciles at dawn.

Gravestone gargoyles grin as grimly as gruesome grannies.

Tina tackled a talking turtle.

Peter Potter peeled a pile of potatoes for pancakes. How many
potato pancakes did Peter Potter eat? A pile!

Musicians miming into microphones make muffled music.

The otter mother and her daughter otter ought
to go to Camp Granada.

In Connecticut, a pickle is not officially a pickle unless...IT BOUNCES!

VIOLENT VIKINGS

*How tough were Viking warriors? Some were so fierce
they even scared other Vikings.*

GUNNAR TELL A TALE?

In the years 700 to A.D. 1000, the people who lived in what are
now the countries of Denmark, Norway, Sweden, and Iceland were
called "Vikings." Why? Because their origins were in *Viken*, an
area in Norway. The Vikings were feared sea-going raiders and
conquerors. Just the hint of a Viking raid could make men shiver in
their boots.

Much of what is known about legendary Viking warriors
comes from the Viking sagas, written in Iceland in the thirteenth
and fourteenth centuries. One saga tells the story of Gunnar
Hámundarson, an Icelandic chieftain who lived in the tenth century.
Not only could Hámundarson fight equally well with his right and
left hand, he was fast. How fast? To his enemies, it looked as if
Hámundarson fought with three swords instead of one. He was
also a perfect shot with a bow and arrow, and Hámundarson was
so strong that he could jump higher than his own head, even while
wearing full battle gear. (Yikes!)

DEAD CLEVER

In A.D. 860, Bjorn Ironside and his men were attacking Luna,
Italy, but the town walls were too thick for them to break through.
Ironside came up with a plan: he had his men put him in a coffin
and carry him to Luna. At the gates, his men explained that
Ironside had died and asked if he could be buried on church

A fully ripened cranberry can be dribbled like a basketball.

ground. The priests agreed but allowed only the coffin inside the church. Once there, Ironside jumped out, fought his way back to the city gates, and opened them for his waiting men.

SNAKE PROOF

Living in the 800s, Ragnar Lodbrok was a fabled hero from Östergötland, a region of southeastern Sweden. Legend has it that when he was 15 years old, Ragnar Lodbrok decided to win the hand of a princess whose castle had a problem: a giant poisonous snake had taken up residence. Other warriors wanted to kill the giant snake, but its poison was so deadly that they were too afraid to go near it. Lodbrok boiled animal skins in tar and sand to make himself a special protective suit. Wearing the suit, he faced down the fanged fiend and won. The princess's father was so impressed by Lodbrok's clever snake-proof suit and skill with a spear that he allowed Lodbrok to marry his daughter.

I'M GOING, ANYWAY

Ivarr the "Boneless" got his nickname because historians think he had "brittle-bone disease," a medical condition that made his bones break easily and left him unable to walk. He didn't let his weak legs stop him, though: he had his men lift him onto a shield and carry him into battle. Once on the field, Ivarr fought with a bow and arrow. In spite of being "Boneless," Ivarr led the "Great Heathen Army" into England and won enough victories

Iceland has the highest percentage of Internet users in the world.

to take the throne of York in A.D. 866. He went on to command the Irish Sea region as King of Dublin until his (probable) death in 870.

GR-R-R-IRL POWER

Freydis Eiriksdottir was the illegitimate daughter of the legendary Erik the Red, and was the half sister of Leif Eriksson. The Sagas say that around the year 1000, Freydis went ashore with her Viking crew to trade with the natives in Vinland (now Newfoundland, Canada). At first the market went well, but then the villagers ambushed the Vikings. The Vikings began to retreat, and some say that Freydis mocked them for their cowardice, yelling, "Let me but have a weapon. I think I could fight better than any of you!" She soon had her chance. The attackers rushed toward her. Freydis scooped up a dead Viking's sword and faced them. Lifting her shirt, she pounded the sword against her chest. The attackers were so surprised to see that the screaming warrior they'd been chasing was a woman, they turned around and ran.

That's gutsy, but not enough to put Freydis on the list of violent Vikings. What was? On either this same trading voyage or another (no one's quite certain), Freydis had a couple of business partners—some say they were her brothers. Once the trading was done, Freydis decided she'd rather keep all the goods than split them. She picked a fight with the other Vikings and won. All the men of the other Viking crew—including those who might have been her brothers—were slaughtered. When her own men refused to kill the five women who'd come with the other crew, Freydis took her axe to them.

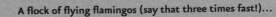

A flock of flying flamingos (say that three times fast!)...

DOGGONE IT!

Here are some favorite quotes about a kid's best friend.

"The best way to get a puppy is to beg for a baby brother. They'll settle for a puppy every time."

—Winston Pendelton

"The more boys I meet, the more I love my dog."

—Carrie Underwood

"I looked up my family tree and found three dogs using it."

—Rodney Dangerfield

"I've seen a look in dogs' eyes, a quickly vanishing look of amazed contempt, and I am convinced that basically dogs think humans are nuts."

—John Steinbeck

"Dachshunds are ideal dogs for small children, as they are already stretched and pulled to such a length that the child cannot do much harm one way or the other."

—Robert Benchley

"If you think dogs can't count, try putting three dog biscuits in your pocket and then giving Fido only two of them."

—Phil Pastoret

"Heaven goes by favor. If it went by merit, you would stay out and your dog would go in."

—Mark Twain

"Some of my best leading men have been dogs and horses."

—Elizabeth Taylor

"Dogs are my favorite people."

—Richard Dean Anderson

"People teach their dogs to sit. It's a trick. I've been sitting my whole life, and a dog has never looked at me as though he thought I was tricky."

—Mitch Hedberg

...can consist of hundreds of thousands of birds!

SLIP SLIDIN' AWAY

How a toy went from one kid's front yard to every kid's backyard.

THE LONG HOT SUMMER

In the summer of 1960, Robert Carrier came home one evening to find his 10-year-old son Mike and a neighborhood friend hosing down the sloped, painted driveway of their California home. Getting a running start from the garage, the boys slid down the wet slippery surface on their feet, before sitting down mid-run and sliding all the way to the curb.

"Jeez, you guys are going to kill yourselves," Carrier said.

To keep that from happening, Carrier, who was in the upholstery business, took a 50-foot strip of naugahyde—a vinyl-coated fabric—popped some holes in it, and stuck the running hose underneath. It immediately drenched the naugahyde, making it too slippery to stand up on. The Slip'n Slide was born.

WET AND WILD

Carrier was convinced that every kid in America would want a Slip n' Slide, especially those who didn't have access to a swimming pool. He patented his "Aquatic Play Equipment" and sold the idea to the Wham-O toy company. Carrier was right: Wham-O sold three million Slip'n Slides the first year. And since 1961, more than 30 million kids have turned their lawns into mini-waterparks with the toy company's 25-foot plastic version of a caring dad's invention.

ROAD TRIP!

Try these out the next time you're stuck in the car and you forgot to bring this book with you.

THE NEVERENDING TITLE GAME. The first player calls out the name of a famous book, movie, or TV show—for example, *Adventure Time.* The next player has to add to the title, either at the beginning or the end, resulting in, for example, *Pee Wee's Big Adventure Time.* Players keep taking turns, aiming to keep the title going for as many words as possible. If a player can't think of a way to add on to the title, that person is out!

POETRY WITH BILLBOARDS. One player chooses four words from billboards and tells them to the other player. That player then has to make a four-line rhyming poem. Each line has to include one of the four billboard words. For example, player one might find the words **pie**, **up**, **dog**, and **next**. From those, player two might come up with this poem:

> A man took an apple **pie**
> And threw it **up** into the sky.
> It was so sad, what happened **next**,
> The pie fell on his **dog** named Rex.

TWO TRUTHS, ONE LIE. Whoever is "it" says three things about himself out loud: two of them are true, and the third is completely made up. The other players then have to guess which sentence was a lie. Whoever guesses correctly goes next!

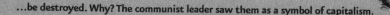

...be destroyed. Why? The communist leader saw them as a symbol of capitalism.

REAL UNICORNS!

Unicorns pop up in legends from all over the world.
That must mean they're real or...not.

CLAIM: Famed explorer Marco Polo saw unicorns in the thirteenth century. He said that they were "ugly brutes."
FACT: Scholars believe that Polo did see a horned animal—a rhinoceros.

CLAIM: Unicorns are mentioned in the Bible nine times.
FACT: The word seems to have first popped up in the 1611 version of the King James version of the Bible. Scholars say it wasn't magic that put unicorns into a book many consider to be Holy Scripture: it was mistranslation and misunderstanding. The Hebrew word "re'em"—which was translated as "unicorn"—most likely referred to the *rimu*, a now-extinct species of ox.

CLAIM: The horn of a captured unicorn, when ground into a powder, has medicinal qualities, such as the ability to destroy poison and to purify water. In the sixteenth century, an intact unicorn horn was worth ten times more than gold. They were sold in pharmacies well into the 1700s.
FACT: Merchants really got their unicorn powder and horns from the narwhal, a whale-like creature with a protruding tooth that looks like a horn. (Poor narwhals!)

CLAIM: In November 2012, the government-run North Korean Central News Agency announced that scientists there had found

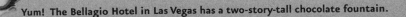

Yum! The Bellagio Hotel in Las Vegas has a two-story-tall chocolate fountain.

the burial site of a unicorn—the one that was said to have been ridden by King Dongmyeong who had founded Korea (known as Goguryeo at the time) in 37 B.C. The site was located near a temple in the North Korean capital of Pyongyang. A rock engraved with "Unicorn Lair" marked the grave.

FACT: Sung-Yoon Lee, a professor of Korean studies at Tufts University, told *LiveScience* that the report is political propaganda. Why would a government support the claim that unicorns are real? Probably to support the rule of Kim Jong-un, North Korea's new leader. "It's symbolic," Lee said. North Koreans don't take reports like this literally the way Westerners would. Another professor said the report was mistranslated. What was found was not a unicorn's lair at all. It was the burial site of a *kirin*. What's that? A beast with a dragon's head, a deer's body, and the tail of a cow. (That makes a lot more sense...not.)

"Good-bye" came from "God bye," which came from "God be with you."

X-TREME TRIVIA

X-pecting a few factoids about x-treme sports? X-actly!

- Who started the X Games? ESPN! The cable sports channel created the Extreme Games in 1995.

- For ESPN, the Extreme Games were a way to lure young people who'd become bored with baseball and football back to sports TV. They spent $10 million on the first games. It worked. About 200,000 spectators came to Rhode Island to watch the games in person, and 300,000 tuned into the channel to watch...every day! (*Ka-ching!*)

- The first Extreme Games included skateboarding, bungee jumping, rollerblading, mountain biking, sky surfing, and street luging. Winners took home gold, silver, and bronze medals.

- Athletes were psyched just to be invited to those first games. Why? Not only did they get to compete, they got free food and were housed in dorms instead of having to sleep in their vans.

- The X Games were supposed to be held every two years, like a mini-Olympics, but they were so popular ESPN decided to make them annual.

- The youngest X Games competitor so far: eleven-year-old Jagger Eaton. Jagger finished twelfth in the Skateboard Big Air contest in 2012.

A baby giraffe falls from a height of 6 feet when it is born. (Ouch!)

- Skateboard Street League champion Nyjah Huston was also 11 when he first competed in the 2006 Games, but the famous skater was four months older than Eaton.

- Vermont snowboarder Kelly Clark was the first female snowboarder to nail a 1080 in Superpipe competition. She was also the first woman to three-peat gold in the snowboard Superpipe event.

- Brazilian-American skateboarder Bob Burnquist competed in every Summer X Games between 1995 and 2013.

- The X Games have led to several spectacular competition "firsts." Skater Tony Hawk aced the first-ever 900 in competition after rotating 2½ times in midair. And BMX legend and trick inventor Matt Hoffman was first to land a no-handed 900 spin in the Bike Vert contest.

- Extreme Sports equal extreme danger. At the 2013 Winter X Games in Aspen, Colorado, 25-year-old professional snowmobiler Caleb Moore tried a flip with his 450-pound machine. The trick went wrong, and Moore was crushed by the snowmobile. His death was the first in X Games history, prompting ESPN to discontinue the snowmobile best-trick event.

- Currently, the X Games happen six times a year. They're hosted by cities around the world. And extreme athletes have been re-named "action sports athletes."

Duh: In Denmark, it's illegal to start a car if someone is under the vehicle.

ASK THE EXPERTS

Everyone's got a question or two they'd like answered. Here are a few classic questions with answers from top trivia experts.

BIG CHEESE

Q: What causes the holes in Swiss cheese?

A: "The cheese industry prefers to call these openings eyes rather than holes. The eyes are created by expanding gases that are emitted by a bacterium known as the eye former. The eye former is introduced during the early stages of Swiss cheese production. The bacterium forms the holes, helps ripen the cheese, and lends Swiss cheese its distinctive flavor." (From *Imponderables* by David Feldman)

DIG DEEP

Q: Why do cats bury their poop?

A: "When you consider that the cat is evolved from desert animals, it's pretty easy to understand why she buries her mess in the sand. In the wild, only secondary cats bury their waste. The dominant feline, on the other hand, will actually display its feces prominently. This sends a strong message of its dominance. However, in today's modern home, you are the dominant animal—and Kitty chooses not to offend you." (From *Why Do Cats Sulk?* by Arline Bleecker)

YIKES!

Q: Can you really get so scared that your hair will stand up?

A: "Hair-raising by fright is a reality and not a figure of speech. Each hair on the bodies of mammals is equipped with a tiny muscle

capable when properly stimulated of pulling the hair erect. The muscles are all connected with the nervous system by nerve fibers, and they can act simultaneously in response. Perhaps this ability to make the hair stand on end was originally a protective feature, but the hair muscles in humans have been dormant for so long that they will respond only to an extraordinary stimulus such as a severe fright."
(From *Why Do Some Shoes Squeak?* by George W. Stimpson)

A REAL EYE-OPENER

Q: What's that gunk in my eyes in the morning?
A: "The substance collects around the eyes because of irritation. During the day, the dried mucus consists of salts and proteins secreted in response to dryness or exposure to pollution. The mucus continues to collect and dries out in the corners of your eyes while you're asleep even though tears keep the eyes moist."
(From NewScientist's *Does Anything Eat Wasps?*)

* * *

WORLD'S DUMBEST MOVIE MERCHANDISE

- *The Hunger Games* cookbook

- *Star Wars* toaster (puts an imprint of Darth Vader on toast)

- *Thor* dumbbell alarm clock

- *G.I. Joe* "Berry Blast" conditioning shampoo

- *The Little Mermaid* shark-jaw gold ring

- *Twilight Eclipse* Edward Christmas stocking

- *Star Wars, Episode I* Jar Jar Binks lollipop. Jar Jar's mouth opens up and the lollipop is…his tongue.

What has six wheels and flies? A garbage truck.

PENGUIN POP

Now you don't have to go to the North Pole to see penguins!
(Did you catch the oops in that intro? See below.)

WHAT YOU NEED:

- pear
- chocolate chips
- cream cheese
- small carrot triangle
- small bowl
- pastry brush
- knife
- Popsicle stick

WHAT YOU DO:

1. Rinse and dry your pear. With an adult's help, cut a thin, circular slice off the front of the pear to make the penguin's white stomach.

2. Cut two wings by slicing a strip of pear on each side of the belly. (Start at the bottom and leave the top attached.)

3. Microwave a handful of chocolate chips in a small bowl for 10 seconds. Stir the chips and continue to microwave in 10-second intervals until they're melted and smooth.

4. Insert the Popsicle stick into the bottom of the pear. Hold the pear by the stick and brush chocolate all over the pear penguin except under its wings and on its belly.

5. Put the penguin on a plate or a sheet of waxed paper, and then put it in the freezer for 10 minutes or until the chocolate is firm.

6. Dab two dots of cream cheese on the frozen penguin for eyes.

7. Stick the pointy end of a chocolate chip into each cream-cheese eye to make a pupil and add the carrot triangle as a beak. Yum!

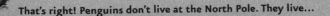

That's right! Penguins don't live at the North Pole. They live...

DUCK, DUCK... SILLY GOOSE!

Can you find the flaw in this bird-brained scheme?

The 13 members of the Minnesota Mallards have flocked across the country for a rugby match against the Tennessee Teals. They're hoping for a good night's sleep before the competition. Each has reserved a room at the Gander Motel. When they arrive, they discover that the motel has only 12 rooms. Two ducks will have to share. "This won't do," says team captain Marty Mallard. "We all quack in our sleep. When one nods off he'll wake up the other. Without proper rest, we'll lose the match for sure."

"Don't worry," says motel manager Garrett Goose. "You can each have your own room."

"How is that possible?" asks Marty.

"Come with me," says Garrett. "I'll show you."

Garret walks across the lobby and opens the door to Room 1. He tells the first and second ducks to wait inside. Then he brings the third duck to Room 2, the fourth to Room 3, the fifth to Room 4, the sixth to Room 5, the seventh to Room 6, the eighth to Room 7, the ninth to Room 8, the tenth to Room 9, the eleventh to Room 10, and the twelfth to Room 11.

"There's one room left," Garrett says. "I will put the extra duck from Room 1 into Room 12, and each will have his own room."

That works, right? Wrong! Can you figure out what's totally quacked about Garrett's plan?

Answer on page 284.

HI, HONEY!

*Sweet name...cute face...but whatever you do,
don't mess with da badger.*

- The honey badger has the body of a weasel and the coloring of a skunk.

- Its scientific name, *Mellivora capensis*, means "honey eater of the Cape." The name refers to the badger's love of honey—yum!—and the Cape of Good Hope, South Africa. That's where it was first spotted by guys who like to give animals Latin names.

- Honey badgers can be found in the Middle East, India, central Asia, and Africa.

- The honey badger spends most of its time sleeping and digging for food.

- Its teeth and jaws are so powerful, it can crush a tortoise's shell.

- Honey badgers routinely devour some of the most dangerous snakes in Africa, including the king cobra and the black mamba. Another favorite food? The puff adder, a snake with venom so strong it can melt human skin. If the honey badger gets bitten, it takes a nap.

- A big cat like a lion or leopard can weigh up to 550 pounds. The honey badger weighs just 13 to 30, yet in a lion-badger fight, the badger often escapes. How? Teeth, claws, jaws, and a nasty spray that comes from the honey badger's butt.

- It has skin so thick and rubbery even a blow from a machete won't scratch it.

- That tough skin protects the honey badger from bee stings. Good thing! The honey badger loves nothing better than (you guessed it) honey! To get at the bee larvae and honeycomb inside the hives, honey badgers will withstand hundreds of venomous stings every time they dine. (Full-grown bears will flee a hive after suffering just a few stings.)

- Honey badgers have a special buddy: a bird called the greater honey-guide. The bird scours the bush for beehives. When it finds one, it leads the badger to its find. After the badger digs open the hive and scarfs down the bee larvae and honey, the honeyguide dines on the leftovers.

- The *Guinness Book of World Records* lists the honey badger as "the fiercest creature in the world."

- How fierce? When attacking large male animals, the honey badger goes straight for the scrotum. Once it gets its teeth in, the badger won't let go until it has castrated its foe.

THAT TAKES THE CAKE!

Desserts aren't all buttercream, berries, and roses.
Sometimes, they're downright disgusting!

- After spending almost 20 years as a cake designer, Debbie Goard was ready to quit. "After the four hundredth time you make something, you can start to go a bit mad," she said. In trying to keep her work fun, she made a cake shaped like…a dead rat. Goard enjoyed the detail work so much that she moved on to a severed-head cake and then a roadkill cake. Goard is now the author of *Twisted Cakes*, a book filled with weird and disgusting designs. "I may be one of the only cake artisans for whom the word 'yuck' is high praise," she says.

- To help promote the release of a horror movie on DVD, British dessert artist "Miss Cakehead" created lemon-drizzle cupcakes with lovely pink fondant flowers. (Fondant is a sugar-and-water paste used for cake decoration). And then…Miss Cakehead spooned on a lumpy topping that looked exactly like vomit. She called the cupcakes "the most horrific edible project ever created" and she couldn't wait to see if people could stand to eat them.

- What kind of birthday cake do you make for a boy who loves animals? Probably not a naked-mole-rat cake. At least, not unless you're Cristy Ballard. Ballard sculpted the giant pink mole rat from vanilla cake, then added buttercream frosting and fondant tusklike teeth coming out of the rat's upper lip.

Most sea stars have 5 arms, but some can have up to 40.

She airbrushed the frosting skin to give it that unhealthy naked-mole-rat "glow." Even though the cake shows up on "ugliest cake" blogs, Ballard says it has become her most popular cake.

- Typically, what's produced in the bathroom stays separate from what's made in the kitchen. But one baker thought it would be a good idea to combine them. No. No, it wasn't. When his friend turned 40, the thoughtful baker surprised him with a gourmet cake—shaped exactly like a toilet bowl, complete with yellowish liquid and floating hunks of chocolate. (We told you it was a bad idea!)

* * *

(REAL) CAKE WRITING ERRORS

Here are some of our favorite bloopers iced onto cakes.

Nothing

Happy Birthday Sheri with an eye!

Best Wishes Suzanne Under Neat that We Will Miss You!

Happy Morther Day

America Reads Appreciates Thier Tutors

Starprise Entership
(on a *Star Trek*-themed cake)

Huge Me
(on a Valentine-shaped cake)

Happy Birthday Adam with Blue Flowers
(on a boy's birthday cake with blue-frosting flowers on it)

Happy Hole Day
(on a holiday cake)

CRAMPED QUARTERS

Five tiny places where big-name authors wrote amazing books.

THE SMOKING ROOM

In 1874 Mark Twain got an exciting surprise from his wife's sister, Susan Crane: his very own writing hut! Twain and his wife, Olivia, often spent summers at Quarry Farm, Susan's home overlooking the Chemung River Valley in New York. And Susan had decided the writer needed a quiet place to work away from the main house. Built like a Victorian gazebo, the writing hut had octagonal walls and a big stone fireplace. Inside this cozy nest Twain wrote parts of *The Adventures of Huckleberry Finn* and *The Adventures of Tom Sawyer*. The tiny hut only had room for a sofa, a table, and a few chairs. Twain loved it.

Turn's out, Susan wasn't just being nice. She had an ulterior motive: The famous author smoked a pipe when he wrote. His sister-in-law had the hut built so she could banish Twain and his constant pipe smoking from the main house.

THE SLEEPING PORCH

Before Jack London became a famous author he was just another poor kid growing up in the slums of Oakland, California. London lived in the late 1800s. As a teen, he worked in a cannery, spent time hunting seals on a schooner, and labored as an oyster pirate, stealing oysters from beds in San Francisco Bay to sell in Oakland

Mark Twain did not graduate from elementary school.

markets. At age 17, London headed to the Klondike hoping to find gold and strike it rich. When that didn't happen, he settled down to write. The book that made him famous—*The Call of the Wild*—shared the story of a sled dog named Buck.

In 1911 London started building his dream house: a stone mansion that he named Wolf House. In 1913, before he and his wife had even moved in, the house was destroyed by fire. London downsized to a cottage and used $2,000 earned from writing a magazine story to build himself an attached study with a sleeping porch to let in breezes. London got up every morning at 3 or 4 o'clock and started writing. His goal: a thousand words a day. He died in 1916, at age 40, on that very sleeping porch. By that time he'd written 198 short stories and 51 books.

THE SHIVERING SHED

Children's author Roald Dahl managed to fill books such as *Charlie and the Chocolate Factory*, *The BFG*, and *Matilda* with chocolate rivers and friendly giants and magical little girls while writing in a shed. The tiny building in Dahl's backyard in England has a bright yellow door and white-washed bricks. Sound cheery? Dahl's hut was anything but. According to his daughter Ophelia, the hut was so cold her dad sat with a rug over him and his legs in a sleeping bag while he wrote. He sat in a ratty recliner as he wrote, scribbling in notepads on a board propped across the arms of his chair. (He didn't like to type.) He kept everything he needed at his fingertips, including an electric pencil sharpener and six pencils. "He would go to the hut at about ten a.m. and would sharpen all six pencils," said Ophelia. "When all six needed sharpening again he knew he'd been writing for about two hours."

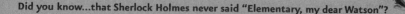

As for cleaning? No way! Dahl liked his writing hut messy, complete with tobacco bits and pencil shavings scattered across the floor. The musty building suited Dahl perfectly for writing kids' books. "I go down to my little hut, where it's tight and dark and warm, and within minutes I can go back to being six or seven or eight again." And that's exactly what he needed to write such splendiferous books.

THE BARE NECESSITIES

E. B. (Elwyn Brooks) White, author of *Charlotte's Web* and *Stuart Little*, wrote his children's classics in a boathouse on his property in Brooklin, Maine. The simple clapboard boathouse, measuring 10 by 15 feet, had hanging windows that could swing open to catch the sea breezes. The walls and floors were bare wood. White sat on a high-backed wooden bench at a simple wooden table he'd built himself and wrote using a typewriter. A wooden nail keg served as a waste basket for unwanted pages. White's only comfort: a woodburning stove to keep out the chill.

White's books show how much he loved animals and nature,

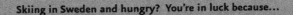

Skiing in Sweden and hungry? You're in luck because...

and he enjoyed most of the wildlife the little hut attracted. But the author drew the line when a family of foxes tried to burrow into his writing retreat. He chased them away.

MR. SANDMAN

Almost two million people follow Neil Gaiman on Twitter. Why? For one thing, he's the writer behind the Sandman graphic novels. He also penned the darkly eerie kids' book, *Coraline*, which became an animated feature film. And, in 2009, he won the Newbery Medal for the most "distinguished contribution to children's literature" for *The Graveyard Book*. Where does this living legend write? In an eight-sided writing gazebo at the end of the garden (shades of Mark Twain!). Gaiman's gazebo is modern rather than Victorian like Twain's. The light-colored pine walls and wide windows surround the author with nature. But it's the gazebo's remoteness that Gaiman loves best: "It's just out of reach of the house Wi-Fi, which is nice."

Though he rarely writes about nature, nature helps Neil Gaiman write by being, well...a bit boring. "Nothing ever happens down there," Gaiman said about the gazebo's surroundings. "I can look out of the window and some wildlife will occasionally look back. But mostly it's just trees, and they are only so interesting for so long, so I get back to writing, very happily."

Gaiman may be a Twitter hero with millions of followers, but he still writes longhand, using a pen and an inkwell. That can be tough in winter: "There are heaters down there, because it gets cold," he said. "I have to try and remember not to leave bottles of ink on the table as they freeze." Also on his desk? A computer, a few CDs, and...a dead beetle.

PACK MY LUNCH!

Hoping for PB&J in your lunchbox? Not if you live outside the U.S.!

France: Cheese, bread, fresh fruit, and salads—but not just any salads. French moms pack gourmet grub such as greens with smoked salmon or guinea fowl over a bed of watercress. *Oo-la-la!*

Greece: Sandwiches stuffed with olives, hummus (smooshed chickpeas), and mayonnaise are a brown-bag staple for Greek schoolkids.

Zambia: Like to eat with your hands? Zambia's the place! Kids and their parents usually eat the same thing for all three daily meals: *nshima*, a type of thick porridge made from white cornmeal. Scoop up a handful, dip it into pan-fried veggies, and…yum!

Japan: Japanese parents go for artistry while packing their kids' bento boxes. Carrot coins shaped like flowers, rice balls shaped like bunnies, and seaweed stalks of grass make lunch a feast for the eyes *and* the belly.

Finland: If you typically slip uneaten veggies to your dog, stay out of Finland's schools. The country's government requires that 50 percent of each school lunch be fruits and vegetables. Two of the most popular options: pea soup and pea pancakes.

India: Indian lunches are delivered hot each day in *tiffins*, two or three tiers of round metal containers that lock together with a handle. A tiffin  might hold rice or *roti* (a type of flatbread) with lentil soup and a spicy curry.

JUST DUCKY!

Before you celebrate, make sure you have all the facts....

GOOD NEWS: A scientific study found that money actually *can* make you happy.
THE CATCH: In the study, people were only happier if they spent the money on someone else. (See…Mom was right when she told you it was better to give than to receive!)

GOOD NEWS: The American Beverage Association says that, with no sugar and almost no calories, diet soda is safe and effective for weight loss.
THE CATCH: According to several scientific studies, drinking diet soda means you're more likely to be overweight and have health problems like diabetes and heart disease.

GOOD NEWS: Scientists in California have come up with a way to create fuel from air, which could go a long way toward saving energy.
THE CATCH: The electricity to start the chemical process that makes the fuel needs to come from nuclear power—exactly what the scientists are trying to avoid.

GOOD NEWS: Math teachers in the Chicago area got a raise!
THE CATCH: If their students didn't achieve better math scores by the end of the school year, the teachers had to give back all of their raise money.
MORE GOOD NEWS: Money motivates—almost every teacher who got the raise was able to boost students' scores.

...and still make sense! Try it!

DISAPPEARING SALTSHAKER

You know when you go out to eat and everyone is waiting for their food and your parents ask what happened in school that day? This magic trick provides a perfect distraction!

WHAT YOU NEED:

- table
- chair or booth
- coin
- saltshaker
- napkin

WHAT YOU DO:

1. Sit down at the table and ask a volunteer for a coin.

2. Explain that you recently learned how to make a coin disappear. Put it in your pocket. Take it back out again and say, "Kidding! That wasn't really the trick."

3. Pull the saltshaker toward you and cover it with a napkin. Pull the napkin down until it takes the shape of the saltshaker. (Stiff, thick napkins work best for this trick.) Grip the napkin and saltshaker with one hand.

4. Put the coin on the table and cover it with the saltshaker and the napkin. Ask someone to say the magic words: *Al-a-ka-snozzle, raz-ma-tazz!*

Hey, sleepyhead! 90% of your dreams are forgotten 10 minutes after you wake up.

5. Lift the saltshaker and the napkin—the coin is still there. Say, "Is that a fake coin? You guys check it out."

6. While your audience is looking at the coin, pull the napkin and the saltshaker toward you, to the edge of the table. Loosen your grip around the napkin so that the shaker falls into your lap. (This motion should be swift and subtle, while your audience's focus is on the coin and NOT on the napkin. You'll want to practice the trick in private before you try it in public. When you can drop the saltshaker without drawing attention, you're ready.)

7. Once the coin has been proven authentic, have your audience put it back on the table. Holding the napkin lightly so it still looks as if the saltshaker is underneath, position it on top of the coin.

8. Count down from three, say the magic words yourself, and dramatically squash the napkin flat on the table. *Voilà!* The shaker has disappeared!

Apple founder Steve Jobs was adopted. His birth father was Syrian.

I SPEAK DUCK!

*Here's your chance to meet some of the voice actors
behind familiar animated quackers.*

THE DUCK: Darkwing Duck
THE VOICE: Jim Cummings

"Let's get dangerous!" That was the catchphrase of Darkwing Duck, the main character in a spin-off from the Disney series DuckTales. He was meant to be a superhero, but most of the time…he wasn't. His mission: to protect the city of St. Canard from the evils of F.O.W.L., the "Fiendish Organization for World Larceny." (A *canard*, in case you're wondering, is an unfounded rumor.) Jim Cummings was the voice of Darkwing Duck during the show's 1991–1995 run, but that wasn't the only odd job he ever had. He'd also been a door-to-door salesman, a riverboat deckhand, a rock-band member, and a Mardi Gras float designer. When asked about voice-over actors, Cummings said, "There's not a lot of us." That's why Cummings has been the voice of dozens of other characters, including Winnie-the-Pooh, Shredder (*Teenage Mutant Ninja Turtles*), and Taz (*Taz-Mania*).

THE DUCK: Count Duckula
THE VOICE: David Jason

Count Duckula (actually Count Duckula the 17th) was the star of the British animated series of the same name. The show ran for four seasons, beginning in 1988. Though Count Duckula lived in a castle in Transylvania and had a sidekick named Igor, he wasn't your typical vampire. He didn't have fangs and (Horrors!) he was a

Carrots have been around since Ancient Egypt, 5,000 years ago...

vegetarian. The voice behind Count Duckula was actor David Jason (real name, David John White). Jason was a small kid and grew to only 5' 5" as an adult, so he followed his dad's motto: make 'em laugh! "It was the only way for little fellows not to get beaten up by the big bullies," Jason said. Count Duckula isn't his only acting job. He's starred in a string of British sitcoms and is such a popular actor that he's become an aristocrat in real life, like the ducky count he once voiced. How? On December 1, 2005, he was knighted Sir David John White by Queen Elizabeth II at Buckingham Palace.

THE DUCK: Quacula
THE VOICE: Frank Welker

Though Quacula didn't have his own show, this blue-skinned vampire duck starred in his own segments in 16 episodes of *The New Adventures of Mighty Mouse and Heckle & Jeckle*, which debuted in 1979. Like Count Duckula, Quacula wasn't a very effective vampire. He slept in an egg-shaped coffin (How scary is that?), wore a cape, and had fangs protruding from his bill. But no matter how terrifying he tried to be, he just wasn't any good at inspiring terror. Frank Welker may not have a famous face, but he's worked on more than 90 films and the revenue generated by his work puts him at number one on the "All Time Top 100 Stars at the Box Office"—ahead of more stars such as Samuel L. Jackson and Tom Hanks. The secret to Welker's success? "When I was little I could pick up on sounds, and then I discovered you could distort what you hear and make people laugh or disrupt a class."

THE DUCK: Yakky Doodle
THE VOICE: Jimmy Weldon

"Are you my mama?" was Yakky Doodle's most frequent question. The friendly little yellow-and-green duck lived with his buddy Chopper, a huge bulldog, and starred in some segments of the 1960s animated series *The Yogi Bear Show*. Fibber Fox, the Cat, and Alfy Gator wanted to eat him. But Yakky—with the help of Chopper—always escaped unharmed. Jimmy Weldon gave Yakky his Donald Duck-like voice, but Yakky wasn't Weldon's first experience acting as a duck. From 1950–1952 Weldon hosted a children's television show out of Dallas, Texas: *The Webster Webfoot Show*. Webster wasn't animated. This duck was a ventriloquist's dummy. The plush white dummy had giant round eyes (scary!) and a bright yellow beak. It wore a baseball cap and a blue neckerchief. If that wasn't weird enough, the duck dummy was born on February 31 (there's no such date) and was three years old—forever. Believe it or not, Weldon and Webster work together today as motivational speakers and promote Weldon's book, *Go Get 'em Tiger (Becoming the Person You Want to Be)*.

By the way, Jimmy Weldon hasn't always been Jimmy Weldon. He was actually born Ivy Laverne Shinn in 1923. (We're guessing it would have been tougher becoming the person he wanted to be with *that* name.)

*　　*　　*

Diner: "Waiter! There's a spider in my soup!"
Waiter: "I'm sorry, sir. We must be all out of flies."

Rhode Island is a shortened form of the smallest state's "big" name...

TV TALK

*And now...for a few carefully chosen quotes about the device
that sometimes interrupts your bathroom reading.*
(For more TV Talk, see page 264.)

"If it weren't for Philo T. Farnsworth, inventor of television, we'd still be eating frozen radio dinners."
—**Johnny Carson**

"On cable TV they have a weather channel—twenty-four hours of weather. We had something like that where I grew up. We called it a window."
—**Dan Spencer**

"Television is not real life. In real life people actually have to leave the coffee shop and go to jobs."
—**Bill Gates**

"In general, my children refuse to eat anything that hasn't danced on television."
—**Erma Bombeck**

"Don't you wish there were a knob on the TV to turn up the intelligence? There's one marked 'Brightness,' but it doesn't work."
—**Gallagher**

"Television: a medium—so called because it is neither rare nor well done."
—**Ernie Kovacs**

"We owe a lot to Thomas Edison—if it wasn't for him, we'd be watching television by candlelight."
—**Milton Berle**

"You go to your TV to turn your brain off. You go to the computer when you want to turn your brain on."
—**Steve Jobs**

HOW MANY...?

Our favorite answers to life's most trivial question.

How many...mobsters does it take to change a light bulb?
A: Ten. All of 'em wiseguys. You gotta problem wid that?

How many...film stars does it take to change a light bulb?
A: "None, dah-ling. The servants will take care of it."

How many...lawyers does it take to screw in a light bulb?
A: How many can you afford?

How many... Vulcans does it take to change a light bulb?
A: Precisely 1.0000000000.

How many... Oracles does it take to screw in a light bulb?
A: There is no light bulb.

How many...government workers does it take to change a light bulb?
A: Before we answer that question, have you filled out form #3927B—the light bulb change request form?

How many...presidential advisors does it take to change a light bulb?
A: Are you kidding? They're supposed to keep the president in the dark.

How many...jugglers does it take to change a light bulb?
A: Only one, but he'll need three bulbs.

How many...mystery writers does it take to screw in a light bulb?
A: Two. One to screw it most of the way in and another to give it a good twist at the end.

How many...real men does it take to change a light bulb?
A: None. Real men aren't afraid of the dark.

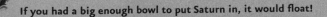

If you had a big enough bowl to put Saturn in, it would float!

CRYPT-I-MERICKS

*Cryptids are creatures whose existence has never been proven,
which means they're fair game for really bad rhymes!*

A **cryptid** arose from the slime,
just to make up a limerick rhyme...
But its smell was so rank
that its poetry stank
and the ooze sucked it down for the crime.

There once was a **Sasquatch** named Larry,
whose friends all teased, "You're TOO hairy!"
He slipped off to the shade
with a Bic razor blade.
Is Larry still hairy? Not very.

Nessie said, "This is MY loch you know.
All these horrible tourists must go!"
So she brought in an eel
whose electrical feel
set those loch-watching tourists aglow.

There once was a little **E.T.**
who sneaked off his spaceship to pee.
The ship flew away,
so on Earth he must stay
until phoning l-o-o-o-o-o-ng distance is free.

Make up your own crypt-i-mericks...if you dare!

In Maine, it is against the law to put tomatoes in clam chowder.

POX PARTIES

Would you go to a party to catch a disease? Three hundred years ago, a British artistocrat talked people into doing just that!

A POX UPON YOU!

Smallpox is one of the deadliest diseases known to humankind. It's been around at least since the Egyptian pharaohs. Ramses V, who died in 1157 B.C., had what looked like smallpox scars on his mummified remains. The virus starts with a fever, then moves on to headaches, a sore throat, and vomiting. A few days later, a rash that swells into oozing pus-filled lesions covers the body. (Eeeuw!) About a third of those who catch the virus die within two weeks. Survivors are often left horribly scarred. Some lose bits of their lips, ears, or noses. So what kind of lunatic would host parties to expose guests to smallpox? Meet Lady Mary Wortley Montagu.

BREATHE ON ME

Lady Mary (1689–1762) was the wife of a British ambassador to Turkey in the early 1700s. She knew a lot about smallpox. First, she knew that there are two types of smallpox—a mild form, which kills only a tenth of its victims, and a deadly form, which kills a third of its victims. Second, she knew that people never get smallpox twice. What she didn't know before moving to Turkey? For centuries people in the East had tried to avoid the deadly form of smallpox by catching the mild form, either by breathing in dried scabs of an infected person or by scratching powdered scabs into the skin.

In Turkey, Lady Mary discovered smallpox parties. In her letters

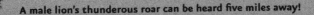
A male lion's thunderous roar can be heard five miles away!

home she described what pox parties were all about. Women brought a nutshell full of smallpox material from the blister of a person who had the mild form of the disease. Partygoers chose a part of the arm to be "variolated." The women made a cut in the chosen spot and placed a bit of the powdered scab in the wound. A week later, the variolated person got a fever and stayed in bed for a couple of days. A few weeks later, that person was healthy again but now armed against the deadly form of smallpox.

THAT REALLY SCARS ME

Lady Mary was deadly serious about helping stop the scourge of smallpox. She had contracted the disease in 1715 as a young woman living in London. Smallpox scarred her face and left her with no eyebrows (some say "eyelashes"). But Mary was lucky. The disease did not leave her blind, crippled, or worse—dead. Her brother was not so lucky. He died from smallpox eighteen months after Mary recovered.

When Lady Mary discovered pox parties in Istanbul, Turkey, She saw how effective they were in preventing the disease. So she asked the embassy doctor, Charles Maitland, to variolate her five-year-old son, Edward. A year later, when she returned to England, she tried to encourage doctors to practice variolation. They refused. Why? Because it was an "Oriental" procedure.

THE PRINCESS AND THE POX

In 1721 when another smallpox epidemic struck, Lady Mary had her four-year-old daughter, Mary, variolated by Dr. Maitland. And she made the event public. Six condemned prisoners scheduled for execution were offered variolation instead of certain death. They all lived and were freed. Six orphans were also variolated, and went on

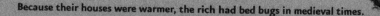

Because their houses were warmer, the rich had bed bugs in medieval times.

to live. She even persuaded Britain's Princess Caroline to test the treatment.

Finally, doctors were convinced that variolation was a good way to prevent the deadly form of smallpox. Even the royal family had a smallpox party. King George I allowed Dr. Maitland to variolate two of his grandchildren, children of Princess Caroline. This gave an "Oriental" practice the royal seal of approval.

THE PARTY'S OVER

Although the odds of dying were far worse when catching smallpox naturally, about two percent of those who received variolation got the full-blown disease and died. Still, at the time, Lady Mary's smallpox parties were the best chance people had to arm themselves against the deadly disease.

And then…along came Edward Jenner. Edward was variolated with smallpox at age eight. He almost died from an infection that followed. When he grew up, he became a country doctor with a special interest in trying to find a better way to prevent smallpox. In 1796 one of Dr. Jenner's patients came in with a rash. She was a dairymaid, so Jenner asked if she'd been exposed to cowpox. Yes, she had. A cow named Blossom had just gotten over the disease.

Like people, cows can catch the pox. But cowpox is much milder than human pox. Country lore claimed that those who'd caught cowpox were immune to smallpox. Jenner used

Egypt's Great Pyramid contains more than 2 million 2- to 30-ton stone blocks.

material from the dairymaid's rash to test that claim. He variolated a local boy with cowpox, and then with smallpox. The boy did not catch the smallpox virus, he was immune.

Because cowpox was used as the injected material, Jenner's new technique, called "vaccination" was much safer than the variolations done at pox parties and by doctors. It was so safe—only one or two people in a million died as a result of vaccination—that in 1840 variolation was outlawed.

* * *

CHRISTMAS CARPING!

In *What's Your Favorite Animal?* by Eric Carle and friends, children's author and illustrator Peter Sís shared a weird Christmas tradition from his childhood in the Czech Republic. The tradition? Eating blue carp on Christmas Eve. Families bundled up and headed into the wintry streets to choose a carp from giant barrels. That might not seem weird, except…the fish in the barrels were alive. Once the family picked a carp, they carted it home and dumped it into a bathtub full of water. (No word on where they bathed while the fish was in the tub.) The kids, Sís says, spent a lot of time watching the carp. They'd stick their fingers in its toothless mouth and even give the carp a name. And then…it was Christmas Eve. Did they fillet their "pet" for dinner? No way! "The children would cry, go on strike, and finally the carp would be taken by the whole family to the river Vltava and released," said Sís. "You would see many families coming with their carps to the river and blue fish swimming toward the ocean." Merry Christmas, carp!

DEATH BY MRI

When does a life-saving machine become an
accidental killer? When it's magnetic!

You may have heard of the MRI machine. But you may
not know that MRI stands for Magnetic Resonance Imaging. The
machines use a ten-ton magnet to produce a magnetic field.
The field pulses radio waves through the body and makes digital
pictures of what's inside. The upside: MRI machines allow doctors
to see problems such as tumors, bleeding, injury, blood vessel
diseases, and infection. The downside: Magnets attract metal.

- In 2001 six-year-old Michael Colombini was inside an MRI
  scanner after a brain operation. When his oxygen supply failed,
  the anesthesiologist ran for an oxygen tank. What he failed to
  notice? The tank was made of steel. It shot out of his hands
  and slammed into Michael's head, fractured his skull, and
  killed him.

- Magnets never sleep. And the trained technician who entered
  the MR room at Hoag Hospital in California knew that.
  Unfortunately, she must have forgotten. Her job? To replace a
  blower fan. Before she could do so, the magnetic field grabbed
  the blower, smashed it into the tech, and pinned her against
  the machine. She was found dead the next day.

- Experts say MRI close calls happen every month. Other things
  pulled in by those strong MR magnets? A police officer's gun,
  roller skates, PCs, power tools, desk chairs, and filing cabinets.

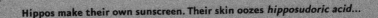

Hippos make their own sunscreen. Their skin oozes *hipposudoric acid...*

HOW THE WORLD WIPED

Before you gripe about 1-ply tissue or paper that's less than heavenly soft, remember—toilet paper hasn't been around forever. Here's a bit of bottom-wiping history.

- The Vikings who conquered England liked a soft touch: they used discarded wool from sheep or lambs. But by the Middle Ages, the English were using hay balls or a "gompf" stick. (Yep. It's just a stick for scraping away the…well, you know.)

- In warm months, Inuits in Canada had tundra moss for bathroom cleanups. But when winter rolled around…they just used snow.

- Early Americans used corn cobs until newspapers and phone books became available. Then they switched. The *Old Farmer's Almanac* even had a hole punched through the pages in one corner so it could be hung on a nail in the outhouse.

- Hawaiians relied on coconut husks to do the job. (Ouch!)

- Ancient Jewish people carried around a special bag of pebbles for bathroom hygiene, but the use of someone else's pebbles? Strictly forbidden!

- Public toilets in Ancient Rome provided a sea sponge attached to a long stick. After use, the sponge would be stuck in a bucket of saltwater to soak until the next bathroom user showed up.

- It's a huge no-no to shake hands or serve food with your left hand in the Middle East, India, and Pakistan…that's the hand people use to clean themselves after going to the bathroom. Right hand—clean. Left hand—don't even think about it!

THE GODS MUST BE...ODD

Gods don't have to abide by silly mortal laws and conventions—and it shows.

THE GOD: Quetzalcoatl (Aztec)

THE ODD: Quetzalcoatl is a feathered serpent (what—you haven't seen one of those before?). Most drawings and carvings show him with a creepy snakelike head and a giant mane of feathers. The Aztecs considered him a god of death and resurrection and one of humanity's creators. According to legend, he pulled that off by journeying down to hell, scooping up the decaying bones of corpses, and bleeding all over them to bring about new life.

THE GOD: Bumba (African Congo)

THE ODD: Bumba is the African creator god who vomited the world into being. Yes, really. Congo folklore says that Bumba had been feeling sick to his stomach for millions of years. (Poor Bumba!) Finally, the creator god couldn't hold it back. He barfed up the sun, the moon, the stars, Earth, and an assortment of living creatures. After getting all of creation out of his system, he felt better and floated back up to the heavens.

THE GOD: Ganesha (Hindu)

THE ODD: Ganesha has the body of a human, the head of an elephant, and an extra pair of arms. He doesn't seem to care how ridiculous he looks. His entire purpose is to mess with your

When two prairie dogs meet, they kiss to find out if they know each other.

life. Commonly known as the Lord of Obstacles, Ganesha is a trickster who enjoys throwing a wrench in your plans and making you second-guess all of your decisions. He also likes to take the easy way out. One story says that Ganesha's parents, Shiva and Parvati, held a contest for their two sons to see which one could travel around the world the fastest. Ganesha's brother, Kartikeya, immediately set out on his peacock, but Ganesha just asked his parents to sit down and then walked in a circle around them. He then announced that he had completed the contest, since his parents were his entire world. (Suck-up!)

THE GOD: Baron Samedi (Caribbean)

THE ODD: Baron Samedi doesn't look much like how you might expect a god to look. He struts around in a tuxedo and a top hat, with sunglasses and a twirling cane. Oh, and did we mention he's a skeleton? It's true. When he's off duty from his normal tasks of fighting off zombies and ushering the dead into the underworld, the baron likes to chain-smoke cigars, rock out to trance music, and guzzle bottles of hot peppers steeped in rum.

THE GOD: Loki (Norse)

THE ODD: Loki is the ultimate trickster god. In fact, he didn't even start out as a god—he was just the son of two giants. But when he met Odin, the mightiest of all the Norse gods, he sweet-talked his way into a home in Asgard, the gods' kingdom. Odin even made Loki his blood brother. After he became a "god," Loki got away with almost anything and played by no one's rules. He

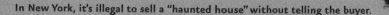

enjoyed cutting off goddesses' long hair, persuading other gods to dress like women, and shape-shifting into animal form. He's been a seal, a salmon, and—at perhaps his weirdest point—Loki became a mare and gave birth to a stallion with eight legs.

THE GOD: Raijin (Japanese)

THE ODD: Raijin, the storm god of thunder and lightning, is too powerful for mere flesh: Rajin is a demon with a body of flames. He typically travels with his mascot, Raiju, a small animal that Raijin can turn into a fireball and launch at innocent passersby. According to legend, Raiju's favorite places to take a nap are children's belly buttons, so Japanese parents always caution their kids to cover their navels during storms so that they won't get burned alive.

THE GOD: Monkey King (Chinese)

THE ODD: Sun Wukong—the monkey god— is the offspring of a pregnant rock that laid a stone egg. When Sun Wukong decided to study kung fu, he picked up some phenomenal powers. He can travel 108,000 miles in just one somersault and can also transform himself into 72 different objects and creatures. Sun Wukong keeps a golden needle tucked behind his ear that changes into an iron rod for fighting. You would think that with super powers he could magic away a simple body part with no effort at all, but apparently some of his transformations don't turn out so well. Why not? He can't seem to get rid of that tail.

BRAIN GAMES

And now...it's time to wake up your brain!

COMIN' ROUND THE PIGSTY!

Your horse, Petunia, was born exactly two years ago. To celebrate her second birthday, you'd like to bring her two apples. But there's a problem: You have to walk past the pigsty to get to Petunia's stable.

Seven seriously evil pigs live in the pigsty. You don't have a chance of getting past them without offering them some of that fruit. The pigs—being, as we said, seriously evil—will do their best to trick you. Each pig you pass will take half the apples you have and then give you one apple back. How many apples must you start out with if you want to have two apples left for Petunia?

WHO DONE IT?

Farmer John's barn had only one piece of art adorning its weathered walls: a painting of a swirling starry night by the famous artist, Vinnie van Gander. One sunny day the painting disappeared without a trace.

"I didn't steal it," said Rooster. "I was hunting for worms all day."

Owl said, "I'm nocturnal, and the two of you are awake during the day!"

"Don't be ridiculous!" Sheep huffed. "It certainly wasn't me!"

If all of the barnyard animals told the truth, which one stole the van Gander?

Answers on page 284.

Not an ideal pet: hedgehogs sleep all day and stay up all night.

SOLDIER BOY

Here's how a duck lost his family but found a friend for life.

ONE LUCKY DUCK

Soldier Boy had a rough start in life. In March 2013, the duckling and his three siblings were dodging cars as they tried to cross Highway 98 in Fort Walton Beach, Florida. (*Screech!* Swerve!) Luckily, they were rescued, not flattened. Unluckily, the rescuers could not find the mother duck anywhere. So they took them to a friend—Capt. Jason Hallmark. Luckily, Hallmark decided to take care of the baby ducks at his home. Unluckily (for all but one), a neighborhood cat decided to have duckling for dinner.

Soldier Boy—the lone survivor—was one lucky duck, but he was also one lonely duck…until…the Hallmarks brought home a wallaby, which they named Pogo. Every day, at 6:00 a.m., Soldier Boy races to the back door to greet Pogo. The bizarre buddies spend their entire day together. When Soldier Boy swims in his backyard "pond" (a kiddie pool), Pogo sits and watches. When Pogo hops around the yard, Soldier Boy waddles after him. They share snacks: apples, sweet potatoes, and corn. And during the hottest part of the day, they escape the Florida sun for a nap in the shade.

SQUAWKING ABOUT BEDTIME

Soldier Boy hates bedtime. Why? Because his buddy Pogo gets to sleep inside the house and Soldier Boy doesn't. "He sits by the back door and quacks. He will quack for hours," said Hallmark. So why does Pogo get to sleep in the house while Soldier Boy has to stay outside? Simple: Soldier Boy failed potty training.

IF GOD WERE A CUCUMBER

…And other weird things folks say in Canada.

Folks say: Who sat on the duck?
They mean: Who farted?

Folks say: I'm busier than a one-eyed cat watching nine rat holes.
They mean: I'm really busy.

Folks say: It's a frog-choker.
They mean: It's pouring rain.

Folks say: Sharp as a bag of wet mice.
They mean: Dumb.

Folks say: I went to a goat's house for wool.
They mean: I made a mistake.

Folks say: Colder than a polar bear's pajamas on the shady side of an iceberg.
They mean: It's freezing!

Folks say: You got me by the sneakers.
They mean: I don't know what you're talking about.

Folks say: Don't poop near the teepee.
They mean: Keep your work and home separate.

Folks say: He couldn't ad-lib a fart at a bean supper.
They mean: He's tongue-tied.

Folks say: Guess that's the last button on Gabe's coat.
They mean: They're talking about the archangel Gabriel, and they mean…the end!

India is home to 780 languages of which 250 are now extinct.

SHOW ME THE MONEY

If you think paying for things with pennies from your piggy bank is weird, how about paying with a walrus-skin dollar?

CAN I BORROW A BUCK?

Ever wonder why dollar bills are called "bucks"? It's because deer hides—also called buckskins—were once used as money. The Chinese used them until they issued the world's first paper money around A.D. 960. And Americans traded buckskins for goods in the 1700s. The weirdest animal-skin bills? Walrus-skin money used in the Russian colony of Alaska in the early 1800s.

BUFFALO BILLS

Bills in the United States feature great leaders such as George Washington ($1), Abraham Lincoln ($5), and Ulysses S. Grant ($20). But Belarus, part of the former Soviet Union, plasters squirrels, hares, and buffalo across their bills. The higher the bill's value, the bigger the animal. But the craziest animal bill ever printed came from the Cook Islands near New Zealand. The $10 bill used there features an illustration of a woman riding a shark.

THAT'S HARSH!

U.S. money once came with a death threat: "To counterfeit is death." Founding Father Benjamin Franklin and other government officials stamped this phrase onto their bills to remind citizens

The number of animal crackers created every minute? 12,000!

that the crime of creating fake money was punishable by the death penalty. Treasury officials have mellowed since revolutionary times: bills and coins now have the phrase "In God We Trust."

YOU'RE IN THE MONEY (NOT!)

The largest U.S. bill is the $100 bill. Zimbabwe's largest bill, printed in 2008, is the $100,000,000,000,000 bill (one hundred trillion). Unfortunately, the country had to print the bill because of "hyperinflation"—it's worth less than $5.

SPARE CHANGE

Bills aren't the only form of money that changes. Coins change, too. Here are a few examples:

- In 2008 the Republic of Palau—in the Pacific Ocean near the Philippines—issued silver coins to celebrate the 150th anniversary of the appearance of the Virgin Mary at a grotto in Lourdes, France. The coins featured a picture of Mary, and each one had a teeny container of holy water from Lourdes embedded in it.

- In 2009 the Isle of Man—located in the Irish Sea between Ireland and Great Britain—issued a pyramid-shaped silver coin with an Egyptian theme. The best part about this coin? The sun disk at the top of the pyramid contains sand taken from King Tutankhamun's tomb!

- Canada issued a glow-in-the-dark dinosaur quarter in 2012. In daylight, the silver coin features a colorful picture of a *Pachyrhinosaurus*. Once the lights go out, the dinosaur's glowing green skeleton emerges.

THE GREAT COLLIDE

Does one good turn always deserve another? Not in this race.

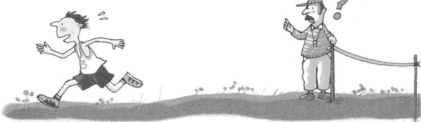

MILES TO GO

In 1981 thousands of runners hit the streets of Portsmouth, New Hampshire, for the Marketplace 10K run (a little over 6 miles). *Pow!* The gun went off and the sprint began. The first two racers were fast—so fast, in fact, that they opened a big gap between themselves and the third-place runner, Tom Derderian. Derderian was no slouch. He had qualified for the U.S. Olympic marathon trials in 1972 and 1976. And he knew his way around a race course...just not this race course.

WRONG-WAY DERDERIAN

Having lost sight of the two leaders, Derderian was slightly bewildered when he reached an unmarked intersection. Which way should he go? Left...or right? As a Massachusetts native, he knew Portsmouth pretty well, so he took what he thought was a logical turn. Several hundred runners pounded after him.

Meanwhile, the two leaders finished the race. Officials wondered why no other runners were in sight. A few minutes later

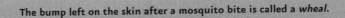

they saw Derderian and the pack approaching…from the wrong direction! Derderian had turned the wrong way. It cost him (and the runners who followed) two minutes—that's not such a big deal if you're at the end of the pack, but if you're the guy who started the race in third place, it might as well be a millenium.

Trying to make the best of a bad situation, the officials turned around the finish-line banner. Then they looked back the other way, in the direction the runners were supposed to have finished. The rest of the runners—those who hadn't taken the wrong turn—were coming, too. Two packs of runners, heading for the same finish line, exhausted but sprinting as hard as they could—unaware that they were headed toward a collision. And it was too late to stop them.

MESS UP FESS UP

The scene was "like knights at a jousting match, crashing into each other and bodies being tossed in every direction," Derderian said later. He extricated himself from the mess and watched as officials tried to sort it out. What he didn't do? He didn't tell anyone about the part his route choice had made in the mash-up.

For 18 years, no one knew what had gone wrong. That's when Derderian finally spilled the story. He told *Running Times* magazine about his errant turn. It would have been easy, when asked what went wrong, to blame the officials who hadn't marked the course clearly. But, this time, Derderian took the right route: He fessed up.

The running community forgave Derderian for his lapse in Portsmouth: In 2012 he was elected president of the New England division of the U.S. Track and Field Association. Now in his 60s, Derderian continues to run nearly every day and still competes. "If the running doesn't kill me, I'll run till I die," he says.

Put away that yo-yo! At least around *linonophobes*. They're afraid of string.

STAR TALK

All we can say is…it's a good thing they're entertaining.

"I am not a fan of books. I would never want a book's autograph. I am a proud nonreader of books."
—**Kanye West**

"I've never wanted to go to Japan, simply because I don't like eating fish. And I know that's very popular in Africa."
—**Britney Spears**

"So, where's the Cannes Film Festival being held this year?"
—**Christina Aguilera**

"If I can do just one-tenth of the good that Michael Jackson did for others, I can really make a difference in this world."
—**Justin Bieber**

"I make Jessica Simpson look like a rock scientist."
—**Tara Reid**

"I love the smell of diapers. I even like when they're wet and you smell them all warm like a baked good."
—**Sarah Jessica Parker**

"I want to be like Gandhi, and Martin Luther King, and John Lennon…but I want to stay alive."
—**Madonna**

"I see everything through a spiritual lens. I believe in a lot of astrology. I believe in aliens."
—**Katy Perry**

"I use organic products, but I get lasers. It's what makes life interesting, finding the balance between cigarettes and tofu."
—**Gwyneth Paltrow**

WHAT A QUACK!

*In the 1500s, quacksalvers were fake doctors. They claimed
medical knowledge but had none. The quack's stock-in-trade?
Selling potions that were, at best, useless, or, at worst...deadly.
Here are a few of our favorites.*

THE QUACK: Violet McNeal
THE STORY: McNeal was a medicine-show pitchwoman in the
early 1900s. Her speciality: TIGER FAT for skin care and assorted
illnesses. On the stump, McNeal told the story of a prince who
had been mauled by a tiger. As the prince lay dying, an assistant
shot the tiger, boiled its backbone, and applied the rendered fat
to the prince's wounds. The prince, McNeal swore, miraculously
recovered. That was all the pitch she needed to sell her miracle
cure. What was in it? Simple petroleum jelly—not a bit of tiger fat.

THE QUACK: Colonel Thomas August Edwards
THE STORY: In the late 1800s and early 1900s, Colonel Edwards
pushed a cure-all called KA-TON-KA door-to-door and on street
corners. The powdered mixture of herbs included prickly ash,
Oregon grape, and mountain sage. The Colonel's Oregon Indian
Medicine Company claimed the potion was produced "in the
Oregon woods" on the Umatilla reservation. Was it? Not a chance.
KA-TON-KA was made in a Pennsylvania factory. Asked if he took
the product himself, Edwards said, "That ain't to take. It's to sell."
THE STORY CONTINUES: Edwards's Oregon Indian Medicine
Company also sold Donald McKay's Indian Worm Eradicator.
Named for a famous Warm Springs Indian scout, the worm pills

A male kangaroo is called a *boomer*; a female is known as a *flyer*.

featured a picture of McKay's wife on the box. The pills were supposed to cure tapeworms. Here's how they were made: Workers cut flimsy tissue paper into narrow strips. They rolled the tissue tightly to make egg-shaped pills. The pills were dipped into a syrup, and then dried until they hardened. As the pills went through the patient's digestive tract, the tissue unwound. When it came out the other end, the patient was convinced he (or she) had pooped out tapeworms.

THE QUACK: Rupert Wells
THE STORY: Soon after chemist Marie Curie discovered that radioactive radium could destroy tumor-causing cells, hucksters starting selling dubious cancer cures. In 1907 Rupert Wells advertised that "If you have any cancer, or lump or sore that you believe is cancer, write me today and learn how others have been cured quickly and safely and at very small expense." Wells had put together a potion he called RADOL. He claimed that it was "radium impregnated" and that it would cure cancer. Wells sold nearly 8,000 bottles at $10 apiece. What it actually contained: alcohol mixed with quinine sulfate, which gave it a bluish tint. (Wells claimed the tint was the glow of the radioactive radium.) Radol was later found to contain "exactly as much radium as dishwater." Meaning...none.

THE QUACK: Cornelius Bennett Harness
THE STORY: "CAN YOU AFFORD TO DIE?" read a London newspaper ad in April 1886. The ad was for an Electropathic Battery Belt that would supposedly treat "rheumatism, gout, indigestion, bronchitis, kidney complaints, constipation" and many other disorders. All you had to do was wear it around your waist.

A jumping spider can jump 40 times its body length.

Similar devices were all the rage that decade "to restore vital energy." They included electronic rings, toothbrushes, and even corsets. Harness's Medical Battery Company hawked all kinds of electropathic products. He believed the body was charged like a magnet. If the positive and negative charges got out of balance, electricity could rebalance them and cure the patient of all kinds of ailments. By 1893 the gig was up. Papers like the *Pall Mall Gazette* refused to run Harness's ads. A feature story titled "The Harness 'Electropathic' Swindle" called Harness "a man of no pretensions whatever to scientific or medical knowledge but [is] a common, illiterate and unscrupulous charlatan." In other words: a quack!

THE QUACK: Samuel Thomson

THE STORY: As a kid, Samuel got a kick out of making his playmates barf. How? He gave them lobelia, a plant commonly known as "puke weed." As an adult, Thomson based his "medical practice" on dosing patients with the same plant. According to Thomson, lobelia could cure everything from cancer to "fits." To cure his patients, first he put them into steam baths to warm them up. Then he fed them lobelia. In 1808, Thomson was charged with "sweating two children to death." A year later, he was charged with the "willful murder" of a patient to whom he had given lobelia. The verdict in both cases: innocent. Local doctors were so outraged that one of them hid outside Thomson's office and tried to kill him with a scythe. (You know—that thing Death carries in all the cartoons?) Soon after, Thomson was issued a patent for his questionable cure. It was widely used into the 1840s. Then, in 1843, Thomson died...after a long course of his own medicine.

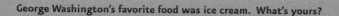

MAKE A POTATO POOL

Ever wanted to make a swimming pool just big enough for a bug? Here's your chance!

WHAT YOU NEED
- a raw uncooked potato
- a clean dry spoon
- a second spoon, filled with table salt

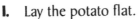

WHAT TO DO
1. Lay the potato flat.
2. Using the clean dry spoon, dig into the potato and scoop out a spoonful. You should be left with a semi-deep crater, roughly the shape of a swimming pool.
3. Fill up the hole with salt and let the salt sink in.
4. Leave the potato for 24 hours. Don't touch it!
5. Did you wait 24 hours? Then you'll probably notice that the little mound of salt in the cut-out section is completely gone. And in its place—water!

HOW IT WORKS

Salt is a *hydroscopic* substance. That means it can attract water from its surroundings. A potato might not be juicy enough to "juice," but there's a lot of water in one. Through a natural process called *osmosis* (which balances the levels of salt and water), the salt draws out the water. And, in the case of the potato, the salt dissolves. Taste the water—it's salty. Have fun "swimming"!

BIRD BRAIN

*Which is a foreign country—and which is an exotic bird? The higher
your score, the brainier your brain. (Answers on page 284.)*

1. FINCH or FRANCE?

2. BOTSWANA or BUDGERIGAR?

3. CYPRUS or CONURE?

4. ECLECTUS or ERITREA?

5. KAKARIKI or KAZAKHSTAN?

6. LATVIA or LORIKEET?

7. MYNAH or MALTA?

8. TURACO or TUVALU?

9. RUSSIA or ROSELLA?

10. SISKIN or SWEDEN?

11. TOGO or TANAGER?

12. QATAR or KEA?

13. SERIN or SERBIA?

14. RHEA or RWANDA?

15. MONAL or MONACO?

16. TAIWAN or WHYDAH?

17. GRENADIER or GRENADA?

18. CURASSOW or CAMEROON?

19. LESOTHO or LEIOTHRIX?

20. MESIA or MICRONESIA?

21. SAMOA or SHAMA?

22. CHILE or CHUKAR?

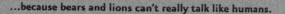

SPY HARD

...with these real-life spy gadgets.

SECRET TURDS. During the Vietnam War, American soldiers left tiger poop strewn in the jungle where they suspected the enemy would be. It wasn't a dumb "hope you step in poo" prank. The tiger droppings were fake. Each had a *seismometer*—a device that can detect ground movement—planted inside. The seismometers tracked and recorded the movements of enemy troops. The devices were never spotted. After all, who's going to pick up tiger dung to see if it contains spy gear?

BUTTON UP. In the 1970s, the KGB, the spy agency of the Soviet Union, issued the Model F-21 camera to its agents. It was super-small for cameras at the time and fit in a spy's pocket. When an agent wanted to take a picture on the sly, he simply pulled a cord attached to the camera. A button on the spy's jacket popped up just long enough to expose the lens beneath it and snap a photo. If a jacket wasn't in the agent's wardrobe, other attachments—such as belt buckles and purse adapters—were available.

STUMPED. The CIA turned a tree stump into a spy in the early 1970s. An agent secreted a listening device in a tree stump in a forest near a Soviet air base. The device intercepted communications signals coming from the base, shot them up to a U.S. satellite, and then down to an agency office in the U.S. where the messages could be monitored and decoded. The really genius part: unlike other listening devices, which ran on batteries, this one was solar-powered.

GO FOR A POWDER. Thief Detection Powder is made from UV powder. Here's how it works: brush some (Don't touch it!) onto doorknobs or anything you suspect might be stolen in your absence. If something's missing when you get home, turn off the lights and run a UV light over the objects you powdered—it will instantly reveal fingerprints and handprints of the culprits. The powder also stays on the hands of anyone who touches it and will show up under UV light.

HANGING UP. Tiny video cameras used to be so futuristic they only showed up in spy movies. Not anymore. After all, you can record video on your smartphone these days. But what if you don't want to be caught filming or can't be there to film? Get a coat-hook camera. It looks just like a wall hook for hanging coats, except…it conceals a tiny video recorder that sends what it sees to a computer. Set the camera to detect motion, and when someone walks by the coat hanger, the camera turns on and begins recording in five-minute increments. The camera records audio so you can hear what the bad guys are saying, and…you can hang your coat on the hook without blocking the view!

CAT AND MOUSE. Be honest. If you're like most people you sometimes talk around (or to) your computer. Well…be careful what you say. Your mouse might be outfitted with the Computer Mouse Transmitter. The transmitter mouse looks like a regular computer mouse and works like one, but it contains an ultra-mini microphone and transmitter circuit. The spy mouse can pick up sounds from up to 32 feet away and relay them long distance to the person who planted the mouse on you. (Mom?)

A: Spoiled milk.

WHERE'S ME?

Before you start correcting our grammar, here's a hint:
Each answer below has the letters ME in it. So instead of fixing
our title, put your brain to work on these riddles!

Here's an example: I'm under your feet when you're over my head.
Answer: baseMEnt

I. Click me to capture a moment in time. __ __ M E __ __

2. Throw me away and I will return. __ __ __ M E __ __ __ __

3. If I don't make you laugh, it's a tragedy. __ __ M E __ __

4. I'm a streak of light best seen by night. M E __ __ __ __

5. When fanned I grow, unless out I blow. __ __ __ M E

6. Quakers gobble me up for breakfast. __ __ __ M E __ __

7. We are the building blocks of all matter. __ __ __ M E __ __ __

8. I'm a cosmic snowball with a glowing tail. __ __ M E __

9. With one hump, I live in Africa. In Asia, with two. __ __ M E __

10. I'm violet, not violent, crystal but not clear. __ M E __ __ __ __

Answers on page 285.

A wild turkey's head changes color when it is startled or excited...

BAD KITTY!

Japanese company Sanrio first introduced the lovable white cat with the red hair bow in 1974. Since then, Hello Kitty has appeared on thousands of items, most of which you'd expect—but a few you definitely would not.

TOILET PAPER

The remarkable thing about Hello Kitty toilet paper is not that it exists—it's that there's more than one variety. You can have your choice of which kitty you want to wipe with. One design features the usual pink, but another is the result of a collaboration with the band KISS. This TP has a scary kitty wearing a black mask and sticking her pointed tongue out at you. Her hair bow is black and that tongue? Blood red.

ASSAULT RIFLE

Yes, that's correct—someone actually thought it would be a good idea to slap Hello Kitty's fuzzy little face on an AR-15. Sanrio doesn't produce or sell such weapons, and you can't buy them ready-made. However, as a protest against an assault weapons ban, a California rifle enthusiastic gifted his wife with a pastel-pink rifle sporting a Hello Kitty sticker.

CONTACT LENSES

You can now actually see love for Hello Kitty shining in someone's eyes. A Korean company, I.Candy, produces a Hello Kitty "princess lens" in eight different colors, including…pink. Each lens features nine Hello Kitty heads arranged in a circle around the pupil area.

BEYOND BAD LUCK

The odds were in their favor, but that didn't stop bad luck from finding these people.

SINKING VIOLET

With blue-gray eyes and long auburn hair, Violet Jessop was too good-looking to be a stewardess on a luxury liner. At least, that's what she was told on her first job interview. She was also too young. In the early 1900s, most stewardesses were middle-aged. Violet was 21. Despite her age and good looks, in 1911 Jessop was hired to work aboard the *Olympic*, a luxury cruise ship owned by the White Star Line. Violet didn't keep the job for long. On September 20, 1911, the *Olympic* ran into a British warship. No one was hurt and both ships managed to limp back to shore.

Next, Jessop went to work on another White Star liner: *Titanic*. Perhaps you've heard of it. That one ran into something, too: an iceberg. When the ship sank, 68 percent of those on board (1,517 people) lost their lives. Jessop? She made it to one of the ship's lifeboats and survived. If you think that soured the young woman's taste for a life at sea, you'd be wrong. In 1916 Jessop got a job as a nurse on another luxury liner: *Britannic*. And (you guessed it) that ship ran into something, too: a mine planted by German U-boats. As *Britannic* sank, Jessop jumped into the ocean. She knocked her head on some wreckage, but—Violet being Violet—she managed to swim to safety. Jessop lived to age 84. All told, she spent 42 years at sea. She died in 1971, and was buried…at sea.

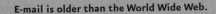

E-mail is older than the World Wide Web.

UNLUCKY NAPPER

Between 18,000 and 84,000 meteorites bigger than a third of an ounce (10 grams) fall to Earth each year. Despite there being seven billion people on the planet, they almost never hit anyone. In fact, most land in oceans. So being struck by a meteorite was probably the last thing on Ann Hodges's mind when she decided to take a nap on her couch in November 1954. At the very moment the Alabama woman stretched out for a snooze, a meteorite flew through Earth's atmosphere and broke into three pieces. One of those pieces—weighing 8.5 pounds—smashed through Hodges's roof, richocheted off her radio, and hit her in the hip. How rare is being hit by a meteorite? "You have a better chance of getting hit by a tornado and a bolt of lightning and a hurricane all at the same time," said astronomer Michael Reynolds.

LOTTO BAD LUCK

In the U.S., states or groups of states hold big cash lotteries. In Europe, whole countries do it. Spain, for example, holds a massive lottery around Christmas each year, with prizes worth millions of dollars. The year 2012 offered the biggest prize in Spanish lottery history: the equivalent of $950 million. Many nonprofit organizations make money by selling lottery tickets, and that's what a women's association in the tiny town of Sodeto, Spain, did. The organization went door-to-door in the town and sold tickets to everyone, which isn't hard with a population of 250 people. The whole town shared the same numbers—and then they won the $950 million. Except for Greek filmmaker Cotis Mitsotakis, whose house was somehow skipped.

A hotel in Bolivia is made entirely of salt—even the tables and chairs!

REAL OR NOT REAL?

Here's a bit of advice when it comes to critical thinking: if a story seems too nuts to be true, then it's probably not. As for this one? We're skeptical, but you be the judge.

TOOT-TOOT, OFF WE GO!

In 1981, the Elthams, a couple from Dover, England, decided to take a day trip to Boulogne, France, via train, a distance of about 70 miles. They had fun shopping and sightseeing until…they got lost. Hours later, night fell. The weary couple couldn't find the train line to go home, so they bought a ticket to Paris. One small problem: they didn't understand the signs or the conductor's announcements. They stayed on the train too long and wound up in Luxembourg. That's not Paris. It's not even France. It's a whole other country that borders France. No problem. All the Elthams had to do was hop a train back to Paris, which they did. Of course, by that time, they were pretty pooped, so they fell asleep and woke up in…Switzerland.

CHUG-CHUG

Swiss authorities were kind enough to put the couple on a train to Belfort, France. From Belfort, they would need to take a train to the town of Montbéliard and connect to *another* train that would take them back to Boulogne. (In case you've forgotten, that's the town they were visiting before things went very wrong). Big problem: The Elthams were out of money. So they walked.

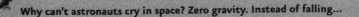

Why can't astronauts cry in space? Zero gravity. Instead of falling…

Bigger problem: when they reached Montbéliard, they were still broke. They tried calling home for help, with no luck. At last, the Montbéliard police escorted them back to the Belfort train station.

Apparently, it was dark when they got there, so, using whatever the Elthams used for logic, they decided to walk 38 miles to the town of Vesoul, where they could catch a train to Paris. They found the train and got on it. (Hooray!) But once again, they misread the signs and stayed on too long. (Oh no!) This time, they ended up in Germany. German police escorted them to Switzerland. The Elthams explained their ordeal to immigration officials who put them on a train back to England. (Hooray!) But the train didn't go all the way to Dover. (Oh no!) So the weary couple walked the last 23 miles home. In the end, their "day trip" lasted for more than a week. "We shall not be going abroad again," said Mr. Eltham.

WHAT DO YOU THINK?

Let's face it: if this story is true the Elthams may be the most geographically challenged couple on the planet. Is it? A few facts: The story appeared in a book called *I Could Have Kicked Myself: David Frost's Book of the World's Worst Decisions* (1982). Here's what we know about the author: Sir David Frost was a well-known British journalist, writer, media personality, television host, and… satirist. A satirist uses humor, irony, exaggeration, or ridicule to expose just how dumb (or bad or corrupt) people can be. Politicians often find themselves squirming in their seats during interviews with satirists like Frost. (Think Jon Stewart and Stephen Colbert.) Frost's *I Could Have Kicked Myself* is categorized as a nonfiction/humor book. So is the book you're reading right now. Reach any conclusions about the Elthams? Neither have we.

...tears turn into a ball of water that just sits in their eyes.

THAT'S SATIRE

Humor and exaggeration—two of our favorite ways to point out the follies of humankind.

"Twenty-two astronauts were born in Ohio. What is it about your state that makes people want to flee the earth?"
—**Stephen Colbert**

"You have all the characteristics of a popular politician: a horrible voice, bad breeding, and a vulgar manner."
—**Aristophanes (Ancient Greece)**

"If evolution is outlawed, only outlaws will evolve."
—**Jello Biafra**

"On the whole, human beings want to be good, but not too good, and not quite all the time."
—**George Orwell**

"Don't go around saying the world owes you a living; the world owes you nothing; it was here first."
—**Mark Twain**

"There are three kinds of men. The one that learns by reading. The few who learn by observation. The rest of them have to pee on the electric fence for themselves."
—**Will Rogers**

"If you want to annoy your neighbors, tell the truth about them."
—**Pietro Aretino**

"You have to remember one thing about the will of the people: it wasn't that long ago that we were swept away by the Macarena."
—**Jon Stewart**

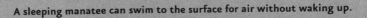

A sleeping manatee can swim to the surface for air without waking up.

CAVES 'N RAVES

You expect to find dark narrow corridors squeaking with bats in caves, but you'll never guess what these caves have in store.

AN A-MAZING CAVE

Kentucky's Mammoth Cave is home to the longest continuous network of caves in the world, measuring more than 400 miles long. That's more than half the length of Florida from end to end. The most unexpected thing about this maze of a cave? Ghosts! All caves have enough shadows and shivers of cold air and disembodied footsteps to cause freak-outs. But even experienced cave guides report ghostly sightings here.

In 1858, *Knickerbocker Magazine* reported the deathbed confession of a girl named Melissa. A few years earlier, so Melissa claimed, she'd had a schoolgirl crush on her tutor. Unfortunately for him, he did not love her back. Melissa led him into the caves. She guided him to an underground stream called Echo River, then disappeared into a twist of the maze and left him alone to find his way out. He never did. Melissa made daily trips into the maze, searching and calling his name, but she never found the man she'd loved and spitefully lost. At the time, many thought the story was a hoax. But many years later a tour guide was paddling a group along Echo River. "The three of us in the boat all heard a woman calling out. It wasn't screaming, but it was as though she was looking for someone."

ROCKIN' THE BEDROCK

Discoteca Ayala, a dance club in Cuba, brings in locals and tourists to "groove" once the sun goes down. What makes this club rock? It's located inside a two-level cave. Rock walls serve as seating areas, and bright lights flicker off stalactites (those pointed rocks that drip down from the ceiling of a cave). There's just one problem with a cave club: the owners have to shoo out the bats before opening each night so club-goers don't get too freaked out.

HOME SCHOOL

It takes four hours by car and an additional hour-long hike to reach Zhongdong Village in China's remote Yuecheng Mountains. The nearest city, Guiyang, is hundreds of miles away. What does this Chinese village have to do with caves? Zhongdong *is* a cave. In fact, its name literally means "middle cave." This is no tiny dark opening that requires hunching over to creep inside. According to Reuters news, this cave is "an aircraft hanger-sized natural cave, carved out of a mountain over thousands of years by wind, water, and seismic shifts." Believe it or not, 200 kids trek to this cave almost every day. Why? For school!

Think that's strange? Stranger still, some kids don't just go to school in Zhongdong. They live there! Around 20 families, all ethnic Miao people, call this immense limestone cave home. It echoes with the sound of livestock—goats, chickens, pigs, and cows—that also live inside. Since electricity and a satellite dish came to the cave, some of the cave-dwelling kids now have televisions, DVD players, and even cell phones. As for the school, cave dwellers think it's swell! "When I was younger, we used to have to walk three hours to school, and then three hours to get back home," said one of the parents. "The new school is great."

HOTTEST CAVE AROUND

National Geographic says Mexico's Cave of the Crystals looks like "Superman's Fortress of Solitude." Buried deep beneath the Chihuahuan Desert, the cave is humongous: two stories high and as big as a football field. Inside, glittering columns tower as much as 37 feet tall. They look like they're made of ice, but they're not. They are the biggest freestanding crystals ever discovered. In fact, if they *were* made of ice, they would melt.

Unlike most caves—which are cool and damp—this one reaches temperatures of 120°F. That's hot enough to kill a human in less than 30 minutes. Before going inside, *spelunkers* (that's another name for cavers) put on ice-cooled suits. This scorching cave lies 1,000 feet underground, close to chambers boiling with magma. "It's a terrible and magical environment all at the same time," said cave scientist Penelope Boston.

Despite the cave's human-roasting environment, Boston has found life there: tiny bacteria living in air pockets inside the crystals. She's also found viruses, as many as 200 million in a single drop of Cave Crystal water. Weirdly, these underground organisms seem to be related to those found in hydrothermal vents (underwater hot springs) near Australia and Greece and deep in South African gold mines. Could there be some kind of underground network connecting South Africa with Mexico? "It's hard to imagine," said team biologist Curtis Suttle. But for now, scientists aren't ruling out the possibilty.

...belong to a man who lived 5,300 years ago in the Alps.

QUACKY CROOKS

There seems to be no shortage of featherbrained criminals.

WRONG NUMBER

The call started like any other emergency call, with "What is your emergency?" When no one responded, the 9-1-1 operator just listened in. On the other end of the call? Nathan Teklemariam and Carson Rinehart of Fresno, California. The two 20-year-olds were talking about breaking into a car and trying to score drugs. One of the two said, "Get me a hammer." Then the operator heard the sound of glass shattering. As time passed, the operator picked up enough clues to the whereabouts of these knuckleheads to dispatch officers to their location. The officers located the young men, pulled them over, and searched their vehicle. What they found: prescription drugs and other items taken from the burglarized vehicle. After cuffing the two young men, the officers told them how they'd been caught: one of them had butt-dialed 9-1-1 on his cell phone.

CALL AHEAD

It's not unusual to call ahead to a restaurant and place an order. But calling in an order to a bank? Not so usual. In March 2010, 27-year-old Albert Bailey called a branch of the People's Bank in Fairfield, Connecticutt. He asked tellers to fill a bag with $100,000 in large bills for him to pick up. The problem: it wasn't a withdrawal from his account. It was an attempted robbery.

"I've heard of drive-up robberies where they rob the bank via drive-up windows," said Dectective Michael Gagner of the Fairfield Police Department. "But I've never had somebody call ahead and say, 'Get the money, we're coming.'" The teller, of course, called police and inserted a dye pack into the bag.

Shortly after the call, Bailey's 16-year-old cousin walked in, grabbed the cash, and returned to the car where Bailey was waiting. Just as one cop was about to grab the kid, the dye pack exploded, further spoiling their genius plan. The cousins were arrested in the bank's parking lot. Both were charged with felony robbery and threatening. Bailey—who was on probation for a 2003 bank robbery—was immediately sent back to prison.

PLAYING CHICKEN

In July 2013, 71-year-old David Biggers heard a ruckus outside his house in San Mateo, Florida, so he went outside to check. What he found: three young men trying to steal a chicken from his yard. This was no ordinary chicken: it was a 9-foot-tall, 600-pound purple chicken... statue. The young scalawags had hooked the chicken to the back of their Chevy truck and were dragging it out of Bigger's yard. The chicken thieves cut their prize loose about a mile from Bigger's house and fled, probably thinking they'd gotten away with their poultry pilfering.

What they didn't know? Biggers had a surveillance camera set up in his yard. By the next day, the three thieves had been identified and arrested. In Florida, stealing a 9-foot purple chicken rates a charge of grand theft. Biggers thinks that's a bit much. His idea of the appropriate punishment: make the thieves repair and repaint the damaged chicken. Then, "They can have the chicken," he said.

The longest recorded flight of a chicken: 13 seconds.

GOTTA MAKE A LIVING

Why get stuck in a boring job?

LEECH TRAPPER

"The secret is to have nice fresh bait," says Rod Fudge. The secret to what? To being the biggest supplier of fishing leeches in the upper Midwest. Fudge's bait of choice: beef kidneys. "Leeches are fussy eaters," he explains. Every year, Fudge ships 15 tons of the wiggling critters to bait shops across the country. He works seven days a week, starting each day at 1:30 a.m. Fudge says the work has kept him in good shape. In the 27 years he's been on the job, he's never missed a day. "I'm an outside man," he says. "I'd be unhappy doing anything else."

RAT CATCHER

Sabid Ali Sheikh considers himself lucky. He has a government job in the city of Mumbai, India, with a regular paycheck. To land the job, Sheikh had to show that he could lift 100 pounds. But that's the easy part. He also had to go out at night, find a rat, and kill it…in ten minutes or less. Sheikh works six nights a week plowing through piles of poop, rotting veggies, and animal bones in search of rats. If he doesn't catch and kill 30 rats per night, he doesn't get paid. His method? First he grabs the rat by the tail and swings it around and around. Then he bashes its head against a wall.

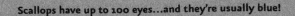

LICE DIGGER

What can you do with a background as a school nurse? If you're M. J. Eckert, you can start your own company: Lice Happens. Lice Happens is (we kid you not) a lice-removal company in Annapolis, Maryland. "You would not believe some of the stuff we find in kids' heads," says Eckert. As a lice remover, Eckert spends her days picking "nits"— lice eggs—from the roots of kids' hair. First, she applies a special foam to loosen the nits. Then she combs out the eggs in one-inch square sections until she's done the whole head. The only other alternative is shaving the kid's head. "Most parents and kids don't go for that look," says Eckert's partner in nit-picking, Nancy Fields.

SEPTIC TANK SUCKER

When people ask Les Swanson what he does for a living, he's not quite sure how to answer them. "We service waste-water-treatment systems" gets blank expressions. "We clean out sewers" makes people take a few steps backward. Swanson and his wife, Kate, are co-owners of Honey Wagon Services, Inc., in Stoughton, Wisconsin. What they do: pump the poop from people's septic tanks. The Swansons have been in the business for almost 30 years. Today, their company's five dumper trucks service 5,000 customers. When people ask him how he can put up with the smell, he says, "You may get used to it, but you never enjoy it."

*　　*　　*

Q: Which U.S. state has the most math teachers?
A: Mathachusetts

TOP 10 STRANGE COINCIDENCES

Call it luck, fate, or chance. If coincidences are good ones, it's good fortune. If they're bad, then that's the way the cookie crumbles. But if they're weird...

1. Mark Twain was born on November 30, 1835, shortly after an appearance of Halley's Comet. The author thought that he and the comet were somehow connected. "I came in with Halley's Comet in 1835. It is coming again next year (1910), and I expect to go out with it. The Almighty has said, no doubt: 'Now here are these two unaccountable freaks. They came in together; they must go out together.'" Twain died on April 21, 1910—the day after Halley's Comet's return.

2. On June 28, 2000, Oregon's *Columbia* newspaper suffered a computer crash. While trying to recreate a lost page, the Virginia state-lottery winning numbers were accidently printed instead of the intended previous Oregon winning numbers. The result? The *Columbia* printed the results (6-8-5-5) of the *next* Oregon lottery four hours before the numbers were actually drawn. The odds of this happening? "A gazillion to one," said a state lottery official.

3. On July 28, 1900, Italian King Umberto I and his wife, Margherita, visited a restaurant and found that the owner, also named Umberto, bore a striking resemblance to the king and

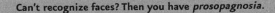

Can't recognize faces? Then you have *prosopagnosia*.

that they were both born on March 14, 1844. The coincidences didn't stop there. The restaurant's owner's wife's name was Margherita, and the restaurant's opening and the king's inauguration had both occurred on the same day. The day after the dinner, the restaurant owner was shot dead. So was Umberto I.

4. On October 17, 1678, the body of Sir Edmund Berry was found on Primrose Hill in Hampstead, England. Three men were arrested and hung at Greenberry Hill in London in February 1679. Their names were Robert Green, Henry Berry, and Lawrence Hill. (It was later believed that the three men were wrongfully executed.)

5. On July 1, 2003, lightning hit the steeple of the First Baptist Church in Forest, Ohio. Lightning striking church steeples? Not unusual. What *is* unusual? Right before this particular strike, the Reverend Don Hardman told the congregation that God's voice sounded like thunder. "That's right, God! We hear you!" said Reverend Hardman. And then…*kaboom!* "The preacher was asking for a sign," said church member Ronnie Cheney, "and he got one."

6. July 4 is America's Independence Day and—in a sense—its birthday. Ironically, it has also been the *death* day of three out of the first five U.S. presidents. John Adams, the second president, and Thomas Jefferson, the third president, had their ups and downs in their friendship, but late in life they'd mended their fences. On July 4, 1826, 90-year-old John Adams uttered his last words: "Thomas Jefferson still survives."

A pregnant woman's body has 50 percent more blood than before pregnancy.

Wrong. The 82-year-old Jefferson had died just five hours earlier. On July 4, 1831, James Monroe, the fifth president of the United States died of tuberculosis at the age of 73.

7. On March 1, 1950, choir practice was due to begin at the Westside Baptist Church in Beatrice, Nebraska, at 7:20 p.m. It didn't. Why not? Not a single choir member had shown up. One person was late because she needed to iron her daughter's dress. Two wanted to hear the end of an exciting radio program. One mom couldn't wake her daughter from a nap. Fifteen people were supposed to be there. They had ten different excuses for why they were not on time.

At 7:27 p.m.—seven minutes after choir practice should have begun—an explosion blew apart the church, completely destroying the building. Fire inspectors attributed the blast to a natural gas leak. Was it just a coincidence that no one was in the building? Rowena Vandegrift, one of the tardy choir members, thinks there was something more at work that night: "It was an absolute miracle."

8. Can a car be cursed? On September 30, 1955, 24-year-old film star James Dean was speeding his spankin' new Porsche Spyder

550 down a highway near Cholame, California. Twenty-three-year-old Donald Turnupseed was driving his Ford sedan going the other way. When Donald made a left-hand turn in front of the Spyder, that was the end of Dean's career—and his life. But it wasn't the end of the Spyder. After the car was towed from the accident scene, it rolled off the truck and broke the mechanic's legs. The car was then sold as parts. Those parts—including the tires, the transmission, and the engine—were involved in crashes, some of them deadly. The last accident, involving a car built on the Spyder's chassis (the frame of the car), killed the driver. After that, the car mysteriously disappeared and has never been seen again. By the way, if you know where that Spyder is, an Illinois museum has offered $1 million for it—no questions asked.

9. In June 1941, a Soviet archeologist named Mikhail Girasimov opened the tomb of Timur the Turk, commonly known as Tamerlane. During his lifetime, Tamerlane swept across Persia, Armenia, Georgia, and part of Russia, conquering nation after nation and leaving mountains of skulls in his wake. In February 1405, he was on his way to take down China when—perhaps luckily for the Chinese—he got sick and died. The ebony coffin bearing his body was sent home to Samarkand, where it was entombed. Word spread that the tomb was cursed. Anyone disturbing it would unleash an invader far worse than Tamerlane had been. Locals warned Girasimov, but he went in anyway and removed a few fragments of the conqueror's skull. Two days later...Adolf Hitler invaded the Soviet Union. As many as 25 million Soviets lost their lives before the German army was defeated and World War II ended.

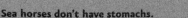

Sea horses don't have stomachs.

10. For 70 years, twin brothers in Finland shared a special connection. If one would get sick, so would the other. If one had an itchy nose, the other would have to scratch his, too. That connection followed them to the end. On March 5, 2002, one of the brothers was riding his bike about 370 miles north of Helsinki when he was hit by a truck and killed. What made this a coincidence as well as a tragedy was that the dead man's twin brother was riding his bike down the same road about two hours later, unaware that his twin had died. The second twin was hit by another truck—and killed. "This is simply a historic coincidence," police officer Marja-Leena Huhtala told the news agency Reuters. "It was their destiny," said the twins' nephew.

* * *

Why did P. T. Barnum lead 21 elephants across the Brooklyn Bridge?...

LOBSTER ATTACK

Part of our work at the Bathroom Reader's Institute is to read lots of newspapers, magazines, books, and websites. Here's a game we found in a paper called Funny Times. (Yes, we keep it in the bathroom.) First, pick a word (we chose "lobster"). Then think of movie titles. Finally, substitute "lobster" for the last word in the title.

Crouching Tiger, Hidden Lobster

The Lord of the Lobsters

Gone with the Lobster

Schindler's Lobster

No Country for Old Lobsters

Alice in Lobsterland

Monty Python and the Holy Lobster

An Inconvenient Lobster

Lemony Snicket's A Series of Unfortunate Lobsters

The Gods Must Be Lobsters

Planet of the Lobsters

Harry Potter and the Sorcerer's Lobster

An Officer and a Lobster

Willie Wonka and the Lobster Factory

All the President's Lobsters

Winnie the Pooh and the Blustery Lobster

Snow White and the Seven Lobsters

How to Train Your Lobster

Wallace & Gromit: The Curse of the Were-Lobster

Kung Fu Lobster

It's your turn! Choose a word and attack some movie titles.

HONKY TONICS

More than 100 years ago patent medicines called "nostrums" were sold through newspaper ads, in theaters, and on street corners. Their makers got rich, but buyers? They just got duped. Take this quiz to find out if you're as easily fooled as your ancestors were.

I. In the late 1880s, Dr. Williams' **Pink Pills for Pale People** were sold in 82 countries as cures for

  a. stomach upset caused by eating a combination of too many bonbons and blue cheese.

  b. embarrassment.

  c. an imbalance of "humors" (body fluids).

2. Dr. Richter's **Anchor Pain Expeller** was advertised as a remedy for backache, rheumatism, and neuralgia. How did you use it?

  a. You rubbed it on your head while counting to ten.

  b. You rubbed it on your skin until the skin became so irritated blood would flow to the area.

  c. You swilled it around in your mouth for 30 seconds, then spat it out.

3. Dr. Coderre's **Red Pills for Pale and Weak Women** were billed as helping "sallow-faced women everywhere" and specifically for "all female weaknesses and diseases." A Rhode Island dressmaker said the pills had this effect after she took them in 1902:

  a. They enabled her to lift a 50-lb. sewing machine over her head with one hand.

  b. They allowed her to walk without assistance after suffering

More deadly than great white sharks? Mosquitos! The little buzzers...

for six years with "female weakness."

c. They made her cheeks such a glowing pink that she no longer needed makeup.

4. New York doctor Samuel J. Carter created **Carter's Little Liver Pills** in the 1880s. They were an immediate sensation, and claims poured in about how a lazy liver was cured by the pills. What was in the tiny white pills?

a. *podophyllum*, a plant root that is highly poisonous when taken by mouth

b. chicken livers, dried and ground into a powder

c. a plant now known to cause liver problems

5. In 1873 nurse Lydia Pinkham used the following ingredients to make **Lydia E. Pinkham's Vegetable Compound** to calm the nerves of female friends and the "wretchedness" of all women.

a. unicorn root, pleurisy root, fenugreek seed, and black cohosh

b. 18% alcohol

c. all of the above

6. **Beef, Iron and Wine Tonic** was a 19th-century remedy made of sherry wine, beef extract, iron, and plenty of sugar-spiking syrup. What was it supposed to cure?

a. "green sickness"—a form of anemia that turned the skin green

b. flatulence and other foul-smelling gastrointestinal problems

c. all persons in withering health

Bonus: Which of these tonics are still available today?

Answers on page 285.

...spread malaria, which kills 2 million people a year. (Great whites: 65 since 1876.)

AMAZING KIDS

These super-talented athletes are still kids!

Sprinter James Gallaugher from Ulladulla, Australia, shocked spectators and teammates when he finished a 100-meter race in 11.7 seconds when he was 11 years old. A hundred meters is nearly the length of a football field and a common track and field competition. How fast is 11.7 seconds? James's winning record would have earned him the gold medal in the first-ever Olympic races in 1896.

At age 9, Utah's **Samantha "Sweet Feet" Gordon** was the star player in her league—tackle football league, that is. Sam played running back on an all-boy team and—with 35 touchdowns and 2,000 rushing yards in one season—proved herself the best player by a long shot. When her dad put a video of her football games on the Internet, Sam became famous for being the girl who could outrun all the boys on the field. She also became the first-ever female football player to get her picture on a Wheaties box. Sam goes by one simple rule in play: "No crying unless a bone breaks."

Skateboarder Tom Schaar from California won an X Games gold medal at the age of 12. At the time, he was the youngest competitor to win X Games gold. He was also the first skateboarder to land a trick called the 1080: that's three airborne spins in a row. Tom pulled off the amazing feat at the 2012 KIA X Games Asia in Shanghai, China. His goal for the future? To compete in all four X Games. "It'll be cool to travel around to the whole world."

The entire surface of the moon is smaller than Asia.

INSTANT ICE!

Presto freeze-o! With just a freezer and a few bottles of purified water, anyone can be an ice wizard.

Important safety note! NEVER USE GLASS BOTTLES FOR THIS EXPERIMENT. Now on to the magic…

WHAT YOU NEED

several unopened 16.9-ounce plastic bottles of "purified water"

WHAT TO DO

1. Lay the bottles on their sides in the freezer, spaced evenly for maximum air flow.

2. Leave the bottles in the freezer for 2 hours and 15 minutes. That should be just the right time to supercool the water, but not freeze it. (If you see ice crystals in them or the water has frozen, let the bottles thaw and try again, decreasing the time by 15 minutes.)

3. Very carefully remove the bottles from the freezer. (Try not to shake them at all.) Though the water is still liquid, it's supercooled to a temperature well below freezing. It's now ready to become instant ice.

Instant Ice #1: The wacko-thwacko. Carefully pick up a supercooled bottle and whack it on the edge of the counter. Like magic, the water inside will instantly turn into solid ice.

Instant Ice #2: Sno-cones. Fill a bowl with regular ice cubes. Carefully pour the supercooled water onto the ice cubes. As you pour, the water will instantly form into a slushy cone. Pour flavored syrup or juice over the top and—*presto cone-o*—instant yum!

Instant Ice #3: The lake of ice. Place a large clean glass on the counter. Slowly and carefully pour the supercooled water into the class until it's about an inch from the top. Dip an ice cube into the water and hold it there as the whole glass of water instantly turns into a "lake" of ice with the cube frozen into its top.

HOW THIS WORKS

It might look like magic, but it's actually science—a process called *nucleation.* Water freezes at 32°F (0°C), but ice crystals need something to grab on to—a nucleus, as it were—in order to form. (Nucleus—nucleation, get it?) Unpurified water has tiny bits of dust and organic matter in it. Those tiny bits serve as the nuclei around which ice crystals can form. Purified water has been, well, purified—all of that stuff has been removed. No stuff...no ice. At least, not until the temperature reaches -43.6°F (-42°C).

Supercool the water to less that 32°F but more than -43.6°F, and just a single ice crystal will start the nucleation process. Once nucleation begins, it causes a chain reaction. Crystals form faster and faster and faster until—*bam!*—all of the water has frozen.

It might take a few tries to get the purified water bottles super-cooled just right, but don't give up. Just imagine the look on your friends' faces when they see your ice wizardry. *Shazaam!*

*　　*　　*

Don't be scared! Killer whales are actually dolphins.

ASK DR. QUACK

The next time you need the answer to an important question, you'll know who NOT to ask.

Q: Why do dogs roll in smelly things, like poo?

Dr. Quack: Because they love, love, love the smell. They're like those people who can't resist spraying perfume all over themselves at malls.

Q: Do crocodiles really cry?

Dr. Quack: Of course! In 1250, Bartholomaeus Anglicus wrote, "If the crocodile findeth a man by the brim of the water, he weepeth upon him, and swalloweth him at last." Crocs also tick. If you don't believe me, read *Peter Pan*.

Q: Why do ostriches bury their heads in the sand?

Dr. Quack: Because they get really embarrassed when the hyenas laugh at them. Why are the hyenas laughing?

Because an ostrich's eyes are bigger than its brain. No one disputes this fact. Not even the so-called experts who swear that ostriches don't hide—they fight when other animals invade their turf.

Q: How do you safely remove leeches from your skin?

Dr. Quack: Why would you want to? Leeches have been used by doctors for centuries. In fact, if you have a black eye, I'd advise you to stick a leech on there right now. The bruise will be gone before you can say, "Help! I have a leech on my face." Then all you have to do is figure out how to remove the leech.

WHAT A CHARACTER!

*Some of the most fantastic book characters aren't even human.
Maybe that's why we like them so much!*

THE CHARACTER: Dracula, from Bram Stoker's *Dracula*

WHAT'S NOT TO LIKE: That pale skin, those fangs, that terrible
temper…let's just say there are other characters we'd rather meet
in the dead of night. Still, we can't help but sympathize with his
predicament. It must be hard to live for centuries and have to say
no to every dish of Italian pasta or slice of garlic bread.

THE CHARACTER: Despereaux, from Kate DiCamillo's *The Tale of
Despereaux*

WHAT'S NOT TO LIKE: Despereaux is a runty little mouse, so if
you ever saw him in real life, you'd probably either scream and
jump on a chair or try to stomp him flat with your biggest boots.
Don't do it! Unlike most mice, Despereaux is literate—he can
read. He's also a music lover. And…he falls in love with a human
princess, which should garner him at least a little sympathy.
Because—let's face it—what princess is going to hook up with a
rodent?

THE CHARACTER: Mr. Fox, from Roald Dahl's *Fantastic Mr. Fox*

WHAT'S NOT TO LIKE: Mr. Fox is a thief, and we all know that
stealing is wrong. He can also be a little too smug for his own

R-r-roar! **There are between 5,000 and 7,000 pet tigers in the United States.**

good. So why do we love him? Mr. Fox is the Robin Hood of the animal kingdom—he takes from the rich and gives to the poor, and he only steals because he needs to feed his family. Plus, the three farmers in the book are so repulsive you can't help but root for Mr. Fox, especially when they're shining up their shotguns to blow him to smithereens!

THE CHARACTER: The Pigeon, from Mo Willems's *Don't Let the Pigeon Drive the Bus!*

WHAT'S NOT TO LIKE: Most pigeons are more likely to poop on your head than earn your love. At first, this pigeon seems to be just about as obnoxious as a character *can* be: he interrupts, he pesters, he bribes, and then he promises to be your best friend (Gee, thanks!). But, here's the thing: all the pigeon wants to do is drive the bus. Is that really so wrong? Just give Pigeon a chance... what's the worst that could happen? (Oh...oops!)

THE CHARACTER: The Wild Things, from Maurice Sendak's *Where the Wild Things Are*

WHAT'S NOT TO LIKE: The Wild Things have been giving nightmares to children since 1963. (That probably means they gave your grandparents nightmares!) When Max first sees these terrible monsters, they greet him by roaring, gnashing their teeth, rolling their eyes, and flashing their claws—not exactly a warm and fuzzy welcome. But things are about to change! As soon as Max tames them by staring into their yellow eyes, the Wild Things make him their king and become the coolest dance partners ever.

* * *

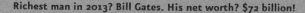

SISYPHUS WAS A SISSY

Once in a while, Uncle John gets a kick out of retelling an ancient myth. This one comes from Greece. Sisyphus was said to have been a king who thought he was smart enough to outwit the gods. Turns out, he wasn't. The head god, Zeus, condemned Sisyphus to roll a giant boulder up a mountain and watch it roll back down again...for all of eternity.

"Oof!" Sisyphus had the boulder almost to the top of the steep hill. *Maybe this time the rock will stay,* he thought as sweat rolled down his forehead. It didn't. As always, the weight was too much. As Sisyphus reached the top of the hill, the boulder slipped from his grasp and careened all the way back to the bottom.

Sisyphus stomped down after it. "Dang you, Zeus!" he yelled to the sky. "I'm sick and tired of rolling this stupid rock up the hill every day!"

"What a s-s-s-sissy."

Sisyphus straightened. "Who said that?" he demanded.

A snake glided out from a tall patch of grass.

Sisyphus frowned. "Why are you sassing me, snake? Don't you know I'm a king?"

"*Were* a king." The snake chuckled. "Now, you're just a poor schmuck rolling a rock up a hill. And the complaints! 'This rock is too heavy.' 'This hill is too high.' 'My back hurts.' What a sissy! If I had ears, they'd be burning with shame for you."

Don't skin that potato! Why not? The vitamins are in its skin.

"See here, snake! I'm still a king, even if Zeus did sentence me to this ridiculous task for all eternity—and, I might add, for no reason."

If the snake had had eyebrows, it would have lifted one. "No reason?"

"Okay, maybe I told a few fibs," Sisyphus admitted. "So sue me." He turned back to his task. "Arrgh, this thing is heavy."

"Sissy," hissed the snake and glided off.

Sisyphus grumbled as he hefted the stone back up the hill. "No snake in the grass is going to call Sisyphus a sissy and get away with it."

The next morning, there were no more complaints from Sisyphus. He whistled a happy tune as he began rolling the boulder up the hill.

"What's-s-s making you s-s-s-so happy today?" asked the snake as it glided out of the grass. "Back doesn't hurt?"

"Nope," Sisyphus answered with a smile.

"Hill's not too high?"

"Not for me." Sisyphus grinned. "In fact, after you left yesterday, Zeus stopped by for a chat. He admired my great strength." Sisyphus flexed his bulging muscles. "He said I was the only one he knew who could roll a boulder up the hill, day after day after day. I mean, look at you!" Sisyphus stopped and wiped his brow. "You're just a skinny wiggling coil of rope. You'd never be strong enough to roll this boulder. Guess that makes you an even bigger sissy than Sisyphus."

"I? A sissy?" sputtered the snake. "I am the opposite of sissy!"

The snake glided around the boulder in angry circles then slithered onto the top of it.

"Look here, little fellow." Sisyphus patted the snake's triangular head. "You need to get off my boulder. I'm on a roll, and you're in the way."

The snake slithered off the rock. "Let me try," it hissed in a way that sounded a lot like a whine.

"No way," said Sisyphus. "This is a job for a king. Not a s-s-s-sissy!" He heaved the boulder forward a couple more feet.

The snake snapped. "If I had fists, I'd punch you in the nose!"

Sisyphus stopped for a breather and looked down at the snake, as if pondering a weighty decision.

"Look," said the snake, "you're just about at the place where the boulder always rolls back down. Let me take over, and I'll get the job done once and for all! You'll never have to push this stone again."

"If you insist," said Sisyphus, and he stepped aside.

The boulder teetered, and the snake rushed forward, straining with all its might against the stone's great weight. And then—of course—the boulder rolled back down the hill, squashing the snake as flat as a piece of pita bread.

The moral of this story: Don't mess with the gods and never… ever…call Sisyphus a sissy.

Drac attack: More than 200 movies have been made about the vampire "Dracula."

TRAVEL DISASTERS

Proof that vacations don't always turn out as you plan.

GOLDILOCKS STRIKES AGAIN

Diane and Donnie Duplissis had just arrived at the house they had rented on Dodge Pond in Rangeley, Maine. It was a beautiful spot, the weather was great, and friends were on the way. It looked like the beginning of a wonderful vacation until…they opened the front door. The place was a mess!

It hadn't been cleaned: Dishes were left out and the refrigerator still had half-eaten food inside. Coats hung from the coatrack, and someone had left lights on the table, ready to be installed. Upstairs was no better. They found wet towels in the bathroom, hair in the sink, clothes in the closet. When their friends Jeanne and George arrived, the vacationers decided to do some cleaning. After tidying up as best they could, the couples settled in for the night.

The next day—vacation heaven. Except the rental brochure had promised a pool table, and there was no pool table. Diane rechecked the brochure to make sure. Yes. There should have been a pool table. There also should have been seven windows in the front of the rental, and this house had four. The clues were starting to add up: They were in the wrong house.

But wait a minute! The key the realtor had given them fit the door. On a hunch, George took the key to an empty rental nearby. It opened that door, too. The house was empty and tidy. There was

Hey, shorty! You're half an inch taller in the morning than at night.

no food in the fridge, and...it had a pool table. They called the realtor, confirmed the mistake, and bolted like thieves in the night. Once settled into the right house, they peered through the curtains as the owner entered the other house. "We were too embarrassed to tell her we were the people in her home."

WHAT A CROC!

In 2013 kayaker Ryan Blair, 37, decided to explore the waters near the northern tip of Australia. He wound up on one of the remote Governor Islands, about 2.5 miles from the mainland. That's when he ran out of supplies. But when he tried to head back to the mainland, an enormous crocodile started shadowing his every move. How could he get past a 19.5-foot reptile in a kayak less than half that length? Blair figured he had no chance. "If this croc wanted to take me, it would not have been an issue."

Blair made camp on a hill in the middle of the island, hoping he'd be too far inland for the croc to follow. For days, Blair built fires trying to signal passing boats. No luck. He tried to paddle off the island one way after another: the croc always blocked his way. Finally someone saw a light shimmering on the island and went to investigate, leading to Blair's rescue. How long did the crocodile hold Blair hostage on that island? Two weeks.

"Everyone's treating him like he's a hero," said Anne Koeyers, manager of the Drysdale River Station in North Kimberley. "He's not a hero, he's an idiot. Learn about the area. Learn about the dangers. There's crocs in there. How could anyone not know that?"

*　　*　　*

SAY WHAT?

The farm animals got into the cider and they're speaking gobbledegook. Unscramble the noises to find their usual sounds.

1. INKO _____

2. OKCC-A-LEDODO-OOD _____

3. AAB _____

4. REYOEE _____

5. FURF _____

6. OMO _____

7. IP-PI-IP ___ ___ ___

8. KUCCL _____

9. HIGEN _____

10. CUKAQ_____

11. OHNK _____

12. WOME _____

Need a hint? Uncle John's farm includes a horse, a rooster, a cow, a donkey, a goose, a hen, a duck, a pig, a sheep, a dog, and a cat. Plus a foreign guest: a Russian mouse who hopped a ship to visit his cousin at the farm. (Yes, animal sounds are different in other languages. A Japanese cow says *mau-mau*, not *moo*!)

Answers on page 285.

ISN'T THAT JUST DUCKY?

In the case of these celebs, "just ducky" means ironic...not happy.

ELMO-NO

Kevin Clash was a puppeteer on *Sesame Street*, best known as the operator and voice of Elmo. When his daughter was young, he was once in a toy store, and they spotted some Elmo toys. "My dad's Elmo," the little girl bragged. The cashier was sketpical, so Clash did his world-famous Elmo voice. How did the cashier react? "Hmmph! I could do it better," she said.

GHOSTBUSTED

Ernie Hudson played Winston Zeddemore in *Ghostbusters* and *Ghostbusters II*...but not in the animated TV series, *The Real Ghostbusters*. He had to try out for the role, and halfway through his audition, the director cut him off. "No, no, no, that's all wrong!" the director said. "When Ernie Hudson did it in the movie—" Hudson reminded the director that he *was*, in fact, Ernie Hudson. He still didn't get the part. It went to Arsenio Hall.

BEAT-ALL

In 2013, Paul McCartney of the Beatles told the *New York Times* that his grandchildren routinely beat him at the video game *Rock Band*. The game allows players to recreate famous songs by playing plastic guitars and drums. The irony? McCartney's grandchildren beat him at *Rock Band: The Beatles*.

Spadefoot toads smell like peanut butter! (But don't eat them.)

THEN AND NOW

Some things never change, but most things...do!

THEN	NOW

Girl Scout Cookies: In the 1920s and 30s, Girl Scouts and their moms baked the cookies they sold from an "official" sugar cookie recipe.

Girl Scout Cookies are made by two licensed bakers—ABC Smart Cookies and Little Brownie Bakers. The $700 million cookie empire sells 200 million boxes a year.

Travel: Hundreds of years ago, travelers carried what they needed in beautiful cases called *necessaires.* They packed the cases with sets of silver cutlery, crystal brandy carafes, and gold scissors.

Travel: The Transportation Security Adminstration does not allow airline passengers to carry on forks, knives, or scissors. Even the carafe would be confiscated...if it had liquid in it.

Graveyard Picnics: In the Victorian era, the idea of locating cemeteries in scenic rural settings turned graveyards into favorite spots for Sunday outings. Families enjoyed either dining with their dead or picnicking on their own prepaid plots.

Graveyard Picnics: Families with Mexican and South American heritage celebrate *Día de los Muertos* (Day of the Dead) on November 2. They visit the graves of loved ones and picnic on flat bread shaped like skulls and skeleton-shaped candy.

The bark of the giant redwood tree is fireproof.

RUFFLING SOME FEATHERS

Proof that fashion has gone to the birds!

THE FEATHER: Ostrich

THE FASHION: Feather boas. You can buy a flashy feather boa at almost any party store, but it takes a special boa to set a world record. How special? In 2007 the former company Ostrich.com decided to break the Guinness World Record for the longest feather boa. The ostrich-feather boa they made was more than a mile long. The company's president, Steve Warrington, called making the boa "a logistical nightmare." After unveiling the boa at a Miss Exotic World pageant in Las Vegas, Ostrich.com sold it in 12-foot segments, along with reproductions of the world-record certificate.

THE FEATHER: Something soft, showy, and bright

THE FASHION: A couple of pet salons have added tiny feather hats that attach with elastic straps to the doggy gear they offer. California's Posh Puppy Boutique offers four hat varieties, including berets and derbies, ranging in price from $35 to $85. According to the salon, pet owners should "let their favorite four-legged girlfriends experience the sensual pleasure only feathers can provide" by decking them out in feathery headwear. (Really?)

The FDA allows 30 fly eggs per 100 grams of pizza sauce. (Yum!)

THE FEATHER: Mamo, a Hawaiian finch species

THE FASHION: In the early 1800s, a ruler known as Kamehameha the Great established the Kingdom of Hawaii. To show respect for their leader, Hawaiian artisans set out to make him a cape of yellow mamo feathers. It took a while. According to historians' guesses, about 80,000 mamo birds were used for the full-length cape, and professional feather hunters were required to finish the job. No wonder mamos went extinct by the year 1900.

THE FEATHER: Ostrich (again)

THE FASHION: A five-foot-tall headdress made of black ostrich feathers looks pretty elegant. But when you wear one to a talk-show appearance (as pop star Lady Gaga did in 2013), you'd better plan to walk home. Gaga's headgear made it nearly impossible to get into the limo waiting to pick her up after the show. She had to bend down and crawl on her hands and knees into the car. Two bodyguards stood tapping their toes as she tried to figure out how to get inside.

THE FEATHER: Any short glossy type

THE FASHION: False eyelashes have been all the rage in the entertainment world for some time, but the idea of making them out of feathers serves up some pretty extreme looks. In 2009 model Agyness Deyn wore short jet-black feathers on top of her lower lashes for the ACE (Accessories Council Excellence) Awards. Imagine a crow colliding with her eyeballs and leaving feathers plastered beneath them. Yep. You got the picture.

Sleepaholic? The armadillo spends about 80% of its life asleep.

SUPERHERO ORIGINS

We all come from somewhere—even superheroes.

SUPERHERO: Aquaman (Also known as Lord of the Deep, Marine Marvel, King of the Seven Seas, and Aquafresh)

FIRST APPEARANCE: *More Fun Comics #73*, National Periodical Publications/DC Comics, 1941

THE STORY BEGINS: Aquaman's life has not been a seabed of roses. His parents were Atlan and Atlanna, the king and queen of Atlantis. They named their blond-haired baby boy Orin. Bad news: blond-haired babies supposedly had the "Curse of Kordax" (an ancient bad guy with blond hair), so Atlan and Atlanna left their baby to die on Mercy Reef. Good news: the ocean swept him underwater. After that, Orin could breathe both water and air. More good news: he was adopted by a dolphin family and hung out with them until a kindly lighthouse keeper named Arthur Curry took him in as a teen. After his new (and third) dad disappeared, Orin took the name Arthur Curry as his own. As an adult, Aquaman has been blinded, lost his hand, lost his son, lost his wife (she went back to her own dimension), reclaimed his rightful place as the king of Atlantis, but lost that, too—and has seen his dolphin mom murdered by a revenge-seeking dolphin hunter.

QUOTE: "I was in the world-saving game when people like Firestorm and Black Lightning were still in diapers. I'm Aquaman, King of the Seven Seas…and I'm the BEST!"

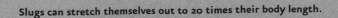

Slugs can stretch themselves out to 20 times their body length.

SUPERHERO: She-Hulk (AKA Jade Giantess, Glamazonia, Shulkie, She-Xemnu)

FIRST APPEARANCE: *Savage She-Hulk #1*, Marvel Comics, 1980

THE STORY BEGINS: Jennifer Susan Walters, the daughter of a sheriff, was born in Los Angeles, California. She had an average childhood and grew up to be a lawyer. But her life changed forever when she was shot by mobsters. Her only chance of survival? A blood transfusion from her visiting cousin, Bruce Banner—also known as "The Incredible Hulk." His radioactive blood saved Jennifer's life but also transformed her into the 6' 7" tall, 700-pound green-skinned She-Hulk. Like The Incredible Hulk, She-Hulk did her share of rampaging. But, in time, Jennifer learned to use her new powers and strength for good, fighting evil with the Fantastic Four and The Avengers.

QUOTE: "I never wanted this to happen, but now you have to learn the other part of being a Hulk. The part where the people you fight to protect sometimes fear and hate you. And it's the hardest part because sometimes to protect what you love, you have to walk away from it."

SUPERHERO: Cyclops (AKA Fearless Leader, One-Eye, Erik the Red, Slym Dayspring, Mutate 007, Apocalypse)

FIRST APPEARANCE: *X-Men #1*, Marvel Comics, 1963

THE STORY BEGINS: Scott Summers had a happy life in Anchorage, Alaska—until he and his little brother (who ended up as the mutant Havok) were pushed by their mother out of a plummeting plane with the only parachute. The plane crashed, killing their parents. The parachute caught fire on the way down. Scott protected his brother from the hard landing and ended up in a coma with brain damage. In his teen years, Scott's mutant powers

How do Cambodians know fried tarantulas taste like crab? They eat them!

kicked in: Instead of getting zits, he started shooting blasts of energy from his eyes. His first "victim"? An air-conditioner. Professor Charles Xavier took him in as one of the first students in his "School for Gifted Youngsters." With the help of a single-lensed visor (that's where the "Cyclops" name comes from), Scott learned to control his powers and became...*ta da!*...the leader of the X-Men.

QUOTE: "Come on, professor! I'm packing a bazooka behind each eyeball. What do you want from me?"

SUPERHERO: Silver Surfer (AKA The Keeper, Silver Savage, Skyrider, Sentinel of the Spaceways, Silverado, Chrome Dome)

FIRST APPEARANCE: *The Fantastic Four*, Marvel Comics, 1966

THE STORY BEGINS: Far away, in the Deneb system in the Milky Way galaxy, a young scientist named Norrid Radd had a problem: Galactus, an all-powerful being that specialized in devouring planets, had his sights on his home planet, Zenn-la. In order to save the planet (and his girlfriend, Shalla-Bal), Norrid offered Galactus a deal: he'd find *other* worlds for Galactus to devour instead. Galactus knew a good evil idea when he heard one, so he transformed Norrid into the metallic-skinned Silver Surfer. Silver Surfer held up his end of the deal until he found Earth. There he met the Fantastic Four and rebeled against his former master. Silver Surfer then went on to fight with the Fantastic Four against villains such as Dr. Doom.

QUOTE: "Tell me, is it easy being green?" (Silver Surfer to superhero Thor after turning him into a frog)

*   *   *

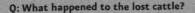

Q: What happened to the lost cattle?

STUPID APPS

Are tech geeks really the smartest guys in the room? Maybe not.

APP: iPhone Blower
DESCRIPTION: Too lazy to blow out your own birthday-cake candles? iPhone blower will do it for you. It starts by displaying a rotating fan, followed by a loud revving motor noise. Point the speakers carefully at each candle, and POOF! The fan that usually cools your iOS device blows out the flame.

APP: Booger Flick
DESCRIPTION: Picking your nose in real life? Gross. Virtual booger flicking? Double *ewww!* This app lets you choose your booger's color and mood (Boogers have moods?), and then flick it by e-mail to anyone on your contacts list.

APP: Hold the Button
DESCRIPTION: The challenge? Keep your finger pressed against the screen for longer than other players. The minute you release your finger—game over. Check your score against the 250,000 others around the world supposedly playing this finger-numbing game.

APP: Bowel Mover Pro
DESCRIPTION: We can't believe someone put this much thought into poop. With this app, you can track your digestion and health habits, and help identify the patterns that get your bowels moving. There are helpful graphs, a calendar, and it can even send a poop tweet each time you do your business.

Haven't had enough? Turn to page 226 for even stupider apps!

A: Nobody's herd.

MONSTER PEPPER

Just when you thought it was safe to eat your veggies!

WHAT YOU NEED

- bell pepper
- knife
- bowl
- aluminum foil
- baking dish
- one cup cooked rice
- one packet taco seasoning
- one small can of corn, drained
- one small can sliced olives, drained
- 1/4 cup shredded cheese

WHAT TO DO

1. Preheat the oven to 400 degrees.
2. Rinse and dry the bell pepper. With an adult's help, cut off its top and remove any part of the stem and all of the seeds that remain inside. Then cut a pumpkin-style face with eyes, nose, and mouth into your pepper.
3. In a small bowl, mix together the rice, taco seasoning, corn, olives, and shredded cheese. Put the mixture inside the pepper.

4. Line a baking dish with foil. Stand the Monster Pepper upright in the dish and bake for 30 minutes (or until its face gets wrinkly).
5. Let your Monster Pepper cool a bit, then try to ignore the goo drooling out of its mouth as you chow down!

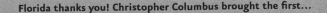

Florida thanks you! Christopher Columbus brought the first...

MORE QUACKY CROOKS

Proof that criminals aren't exactly the sharpest crayons in the box.

HOT WHEELS

Maybe Jamie Craft should have called a cab. Police say the 29-year-old Jonesboro, Arkansas, woman slammed her Pontiac into a mobile home. Then she fled the scene of the accident driving…a child's battery-operated Power Wheels truck. Craft was charged with public intoxication, refusal to submit, disorderly conduct, leaving the scene of an accident with property damage, and driving with a cancelled, suspended, or revoked license. If that's not quacked enough, at the time of her attempted flight via Power Wheels, Craft wasn't wearing shoes…or pants.

CLEANING UP

Todd Herburg and Scott Luker weren't a couple of teens when they tried to pull off a heist in Cottonwood Heights, Utah. Herburg was 53 and Luker, 55. Why tell you their ages? Because it's hard to believe two grown criminals couldn't come up with a more lucrative robbery. Their plan? Use their shop vac to suck the coins out of a car wash's coin-operated vacuum cleaner. The two crooks rigged their shop vac to an inverter inside their Jeep SUV and had been vacuuming up coins for about 12 minutes when they were spotted by police officer Gary Young. "Most thieves just use a crowbar," said Sgt. Young. How much could Herburg and Luker have gotten away with? According to Young, at most, $30.

A MISTAKEN ACCOUNT

When Daniel E. Rahynes came into Pennsylvania's Harrisburg Metro Bank one afternoon in March 2011, tellers thought he wanted to open a bank account. They asked for two forms of identification, which he handed over. Then they asked him to fill out an application. He starting doing that, too. Who knows? Maybe the bank was offering a free Kindle or a cash bonus for opening an account. Whatever distracted Rahynes, it was enough to make him forget why he'd come to the bank: to rob it. When he came to his senses, he stopped filling out the application and said, "I made a mistake. I'm here to rob the bank." Rahynes made off with a small bundle of cash, but he didn't get far. The information he'd given tellers was all police needed to issue a warrant for his arrest, which took place a few hours later…after he'd caused not one but *two* traffic accidents.

*　　*　　*

UNCLE JOHN'S QUICK QUACKS!

Q: What happens if you take the school bus home?
A: The police make you bring it back.

Q: Which school contest does the skunk always win?
A: The smelling bee!

Q: Does your teacher write with her left or right hand?

A: Neither one. She writes with a pencil.

Substitute Teacher: Are you chewing gum?
Student: No, I'm Josh Halliday.

Q: Why was the clock banned from the school library?
A: It tocked too much.

Fairyflies, the world's smallest insects, are no bigger than the tip of a fine-tip pen.

NUMBER 1 GAME

Who's number 1? Who's number 1? Hailstone numbers!

THE SEED OF A GAME

Hail forms around a nucleus—"a seed"—such as a water droplet, a bit of dirt, or even a bug that gets carried up into the upper atmosphere by a storm's updrafts. As hailstone seeds float up and down in the clouds, they become coated by layers of ice until they are heavy enough to fall to the ground. (*Plunk!*) In the hailstone numbers game, the seed *number* grows bigger and smaller (like hail going up and down) until it falls down to "Earth"—the number 1.

HOW TO PLAY

1. Choose a positive number (a number greater than zero). This is called the "seed."

2. If the seed number chosen is even, divide that number by 2 and you'll have the next number in the sequence. If that number is also even, divide it by 2, and so on until you hit an odd number, or "Earth"—the number 1.

3. If the seed is odd—or if your number sequence hits an odd number—multiply by three and ADD one.

> Here's an example with the even seed number 6:
>
> $6 \div 2 = 3, 3 \times 3 + 1 = 10, 5 \times 3 + 1 = 16,$
> $16 \div 2 = 8, 8 \div 2 = 4, 4 \div 2 = 2,$
> $2 \div 2 = 1$
>
> Start with the odd seed number 7, you get this sequence: **7, 22, 11, 34, 17, 52, 26, 13, 40, 20, 10, 5, 16, 8, 4, 2, 1**

NOTE: If you follow the pattern (divide by 2 for even numbers or multiply by 3 and add 1 for odd numbers) you'll always end up with 1. That's it! Now choose your seed number (as big as you dare) and start dropping hailstones!

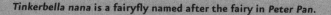

Tinkerbella nana is a fairyfly named after the fairy in Peter Pan.

SPOKESANIMALS

These pets are better at selling things than most salesmen!

AD ANIMAL: Morris the Cat, known for being a very finicky eater

PRODUCT: 9Lives brand cat food, Del Monte Foods

A STAR IS BORN: In 1968 staff members at the Hinsdale Humane Soceity in Hinsdale, Illinois, called up animal trainer Bob Martwick. They told Martwick about a special stray that had come in—an orange-tabby tomcat with an unusual disposition that was, unfortunately, about to be put down. In fact, he had only 20 minutes to live. Martwick hurried over to take a look and decided the stray had star potential. He took Morris to a casting call for a 9Lives commercial. How'd he do? "He walked right up to the art director, the big cheese, and bumped him in the head," Martwick said. Then Morris sat back, as aloof as…well…a star. "This is the

Clark Gable of cats," the art director announced.

Martwick finds it hard to believe that a $5 stray from an Illinois humane-society pound became a national hero, but that's what happened. Over the next ten years, Morris starred in nearly 60 commercials. *US Magazine* named Morris "Animal Star of the Year" three years in a row. He hosted a primetime TV special spotlighting amazing and heroic pets, and guested on *Good Morning America, Lifestyles of the Rich and Famous,* and *The Oprah Winfrey Show.* Morris died at the ripe old cat age of 19 and Martwick buried his longtime friend on the grounds of the home they'd shared. His lookalike understudy took over as the "reigning" Morris, and each Morris in turn has been adopted from a shelter.

AD ANIMAL: Lady Greyhound
PRODUCT: Greyhound Bus lines
A STAR IS BORN: In 1957 a playful 10-pound greyhound pup made her first TV appearance on a popular variety program called *The Steve Allen Show.* Far from being a shelter dog, the white-and-gold, black-eyed little greyhound was a purebred from Kansas. Her dam (mom): Little Shamrock. Her sire (dad): Happy Yet. Registered with the National Coursing Society, the greyhound pup hailed from Clay Center, Kansas. The awkward puppy grew into a 58-pound queen of the road, known as Lady Greyhound who was the national spokesdog of Greyhound Bus lines. No word if Lady G. traveled by bus, but she did travel across the country 50 times, averaging about 25,000 miles a year. One of her favorite gigs: opening new bus terminals by biting through dog-biscuit ribbons. Once crowned Queen of National Dog week, Lady Greyhound never went anywhere without her tiara and rhinestone collar.

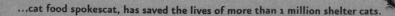

AD ANIMAL: Tige (short for Tiger)

PRODUCT: Buster Brown shoes

A STAR IS BORN: In 1904 a successful St. Louis shoemaker named George Warren Brown decided his company needed to sell more kids' shoes. Brown bought a license to use characters from a popular comic strip: Buster Brown. The strip featured two main characters: Tige, an American pit bull Terrier, and his owner, a bratty rich kid named Buster Brown. Buster sported a wide saucer-rimmed red hat and wore a floppy blue bow tied at his neck. Tige had a mouthful of pointy teeth and was prone to biting. The shoe manufacturer gave Buster and Tige their own radio show with the motto "Kids only. Fun." They also sent a costumed Buster Brown character and a real dog—trained to untie kids' shoes if they weren't wearing Buster Browns—on the road. From 1904 to 1930 the duo put on shows in theaters Brown rented, told jokes on street corners, and visited department and shoe stores...anything to sell more shoes. Once television arrived, the duo became even more famous. Most American kids of the time would have known the ad line, "That's my dog, Tige. He lives in a shoe. I'm Buster Brown. Look for me in there, too." The ad campaign starring Tige and Buster made Buster Brown shoes the best-selling kids' shoes in the country. Believe it or not, Buster Brown shoes are still being sold. The company is worth billions.

AD ANIMAL: Bullseye

PRODUCT: Target stores

A STAR IS BORN: Bullseye, the white bull terrier with the red target painted over its left eye, has been turning heads as Target department store's mascot since 1999. The original Bullseye was an English bull terrier named Arielle, nicknamed "Smudgie" for what often happened to her red "target" makeup. The latest terrier to take the role is owned by David McMillan. McMillan founded World Wide Movie Animals and trains animals for movies and commercials. When Bullseye isn't in front of a camera, she's at home at McMillan's ranch near Los Angeles and has "about twenty playmates that she runs around with." When on the road promoting Target, Bullseye travels with a trainer and her own makeup artist (to apply those red circles). The paint used is nontoxic, vegetable-based, and approved by the American Humane Association.

Bullseye has a rock-star-style contract that spells out working conditions. She must have a private space to which she can retreat and a mandated number of breaks per hour. (How many? Target keeps that info hush-hush.) Like most stars, Bullseye hangs out with other celebrities and has been spotted with Cameron Diaz, Salma Hayek, Willow Smith, and Josh Hutcherson. According to MacMillan, Bullseye loves eating, licking people's hands and faces, getting scratched behind the ears, running in circles and barking, and tearing up stuffed toys that come from Target stores (of course).

*　　*　　*

"The administration does not support blowing up planets."
—**Paul Shawcross**
[White House Office of Management and Budget, rejecting a viral petition for the creation of a national-defense "Death Star"]

...they're clustered together, so they look like one big eye.

I AIN'T AFRAID OF NO...

Match the numbered statements with the related fears.

1. "A hike! In the woods? That's nuts!"

2. "Chores? Mom! That's just cruel!"

3. "I'm never taking a bath and you can't make me!"

4. "Okay. I admit it. I'm the only fox in our den who has never raided a henhouse."

5. "No way am I gonna sit in a classroom with thirty other kids!"

6. "Dad, please! You have to grow your beard back."

7. "Oh, my gosh! It's the town mayor. Hide me, quick!"

8. "If you make me watch *Jurassic Park* one more time, I'm calling a lawyer."

9. "I ordered a dozen donuts. Not a baker's dozen. Take one of these back!"

a. *ornithoscelidaphobia:* fear of dinosaurs

b. *ergophobia:* fear of work

c. *triskaidekaphobia:* fear of 13

d. *politicophobia:* fear of politicians

e. *dendrophobia:* fear of trees

f. *dishabilophobia:* fear of undressing

g. *alektorophobia:* fear of chickens

h. *koinoniphobia:* fear of a room full of people

i. *geniophobia:* fear of chins

Answers on page 285.

In 2014 a leopard invaded a hospital in India and terrorized patients for 12 hours.

HUNGER GAMES TRIVIA

The popular Hunger Games books and movies are set in the future, but what happens in the Games is firmly rooted in the past.

- One night, children's book author Suzanne Collins went to bed exhausted and started channel surfing. "I was flipping through images on reality television where these young people were competing for a million dollars. Then I was seeing footage from the Iraq war." In her tired state, the images began to blur "in a very unsettling way." They gave Collins the idea for Katniss Everdeen, a 16-year-old cross between a kill-or-die gladiator and a reality TV star with a personal stylist.

- Collins's Panem isn't the first vengeful state to send young people to be slaughtered. She got the idea from the Greek myth of Theseus and the Minotaur (see page 169). In that story, seven boys and seven girls are sacrificed to save Athens.

- Like Panem, the Roman Empire had a wealthy class wholly supported by the labor of others. About a third of those under Rome's control were slaves. Slave labor is free, so those who weren't slaves could not find work to feed themselves or their families. If the rich wanted to keep their posh lifestyles, they had to keep the hungry masses under control.

- Enter: *panem et circenses*—"bread and circuses." *Panem* was the bread or grain distributed by the government to the poor. The "circuses" were public spectacles, some of which forced trained slaves known as "gladiators" to fight to the death.

- Collins modelled the Hunger Games after Rome's gladiatorial contests, Panem's "districts" after the provinces Rome divided conquered states into, and "peacekeepers" after the troops Rome left in each province in case of trouble.

- The 1960 movie *Spartacus*, starring Kirk Douglas as a rebellious Roman slave, also inspired Collins. Spartacus was a real person. He was born free around 109 B.C. But he deserted the Roman army, became an outlaw, and—when he was captured—a slave. The slaver who bought Spartacus sent him to gladiator school for training. Bad idea: He got hold of kitchen knives and led an escape of about 70 gladiators. Spartacus went on to raise an army of 90,000 men and start a revolution that became known as the Gladiatorial Wars.

- Like Katniss Everdeen, Spartacus didn't set out to start a rebellion. He just wanted to save his own skin. When Rome captured and executed his chief aide (a man named Crixus), Spartacus acted a lot like President Coin, head of the rebellion in *The Mockingjay*, the final Hunger Games book. Spartacus wanted Rome (the Capital) to pay. To avenge Crixus, he had 300 of his war prisoners fight in pairs to the death.

- The Greek biographer Plutarch (around A.D. 45–120) also influenced Collins. Plutarch wrote, "The mind is not a vessel to be filled but a fire to be kindled." Plutarch has been described as "intelligent and urbane," someone who sees the complexity of human nature. You might recognize the historical Plutarch in Collins's Plutarch Heavensbee, head game maker in *Catching Fire*.

"I don't write about adolescents. I write about war for adolescents."

—**Suzanne Collins**

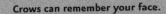

Crows can remember your face.

NO SECONDS!

Don't like your school lunch? This kid did something about it!

BE-TRAYED BY LUNCH

Nine-year-old Martha Payne of Lochgilphead, Scotland, hated her school's lunches. Day after day she looked at the small portions of unhealthy-looking foods on her tray and went—yuck! But she yakked it down because she had to eat something to make it through the day.

After eating, Martha was usually still hungry, so she complained to her dad. At first, her dad blew the whole thing off. "I was dismissing it as her being a growing girl," Dave Payne said later. With no help on the home front, Martha decided to start a blog. Its name, "NeverSeconds," pretty much says it all.

Martha blogs under the name "Veg." Her dad said she should call herself *Veritas Ex Gustu* ("truth from tasting" in Latin). Martha's response: "Who knows Latin?"

BLECH-O-METER

From the beginning, Veg's NeverSeconds entries included photos of her lunches. One of the first photos showed a small piece of pizza, a single potato croquette (a fried mashed potato stick), a few dozen kernels of corn, and a muffin. "I'm a growing kid," Martha wrote. "I need to concentrate all afternoon. I can't do it on one croquette." In each blog post, Martha provides a pic and a rating list:

Food-o-meter—I to 10 ranking of her lunch

Mouthfuls—Veg's way of judging portion size

Courses—Starter/main or main/dessert

Health Rating—From I to 10

Price—Usually £2 (about $3.32 U.S.)

Pieces of hair—On her first blog post, Veg wrote, "It won't happen, will it?" Guess what? It did. Once she found two hairs in one meal. (Double yuck!)

SCHOOL BOARD SMACKDOWN

Martha's blog quickly gained a following, and she encouraged other kids to take photos of their school meals to share. Then, just six weeks after NeverSeconds began, a Scottish newspaper published a story about the blog with the header "Time to fire the dinner ladies." (In Scotland, lunch is called dinner). The school board council at Martha's school freaked out. How dare this kid spread negative images and opinions about school lunches online? And those poor dinner ladies! Council members said that the newspaper article led them to "fear for their jobs."

After the article was published, Martha was taken out of her math class and told by her teacher that she could no longer take photos of the school-provided food and put them on her blog. Martha explained the situation to her readers and said she would have to stop writing the blog. Think that was the end? No way! The NeverSeconds community fought back. Supporters from around the world wrote to the school board to say that they believed this new rule was unfair. It took just a day for the board to backpedal and let Martha go back to posting food pictures and reviews.

EAT MY LUNCH!

In time, dinners at Martha's school got "nicer and much bigger."
Veg is pretty sure her blog had something to do with it. But that's
not the biggest news coming out of NeverSeconds. More than
10 million people have read the school lunch blog, and as of this
writing they've raised more than £131,000 (about $217,000 U.S.)
for a Scottish charity called Mary's Meals. Mary's Meals feeds
hungry children around the world. In 2014 they built a kitchen in
honor of the Friends of NeverSeconds at Lirangwe Primary School
in Malawi, Africa. With the money Martha's followers donated, the
kitchen can feed around 2,000 kids every day for a year.

Martha and her family traveled to Malawi to visit the school.
She met lots of kids, including Ben, a boy who wants to be a
doctor someday. Ben told her that the *likuni phala* (a nutrient-rich
maize-based porridge) the new kitchen cooks up gives him enough
energy to learn. After her own school lunch experience, that's
something Martha could understand.

At lunchtime, Martha became a "dinner lady," helping to
dish *likuni phala* into kids' mugs. She noticed that one brother
and sister shared a mug. They planned to take the second mug
of porridge home to their mom. "Everyone is so hungry," Martha
later told *The Telegraph* newspaper. "I didn't cry once at the
school because everyone was looking at me, but when I got home I
couldn't stop thinking of the children."

Want to be a part of the school lunch solution for hungry kids?
Talk to your parents about donating to Mary's Meals—justgiving.
com/neverseconds.

Homing pigeons have been used to carry secret messages during wars.

BANNED!

Uncle John says, please leave your Ginsu knives, your pet boa constrictor, and your supersoaker water gun at home.
As for these items...geesh. They gotta be kidding!

DEFEETED

In 2012 the Pottstown Middle School outside Philadelphia, Pennsylvania, banned something the school principal thought was a real threat: UGG boots. Huh? Here's the thing: students were hiding their cell phones—and everything else but the kitchen sink—inside the roomy boots. Students can still wear their fuzz-lined boots to school, but they have to change into sneakers or lace-up shoes before entering a classroom. One parent pointed out that pants pockets make pretty good hiding places, too: "Ban their clothes and make them go to school naked," she wrote on the local newspaper's Facebook page.

GOT MILK?

The Department of Agriculture—which brought you the tasty national school lunch program—recommends that schools no longer serve...whole milk. Low-fat (unflavored) or nonfat (flavored or unflavored) milk is still okay with the USDA, but with about a third of kids ages 6 to 19 years old now overweight or obese, the federal agency worries that whole milk has too much fat in it to be healthy. "If we don't contain obesity in this country it's going to eat us alive," said Agriculture Secretary Tom Vilsack.

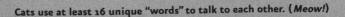

Cats use at least 16 unique "words" to talk to each other. (*Meow!*)

WAR OF THE WORDS

Public schools in New York City can no longer use "upsetting words" in standardized tests. (As if the tests aren't upsetting enough already…) The NYC Department of Education banned 50 words and topics for fear the words could "appear biased" or "evoke unpleasant emotions" in students who need to concentrate on their tests without other thoughts getting in the way. The banned topics include dinosaurs (a reference to evolution), birthdays (Jehovah's Witnesses don't celebrate them), Halloween (refers to a pagan holiday), divorce and terrorism (may bring back bad memories), vermin (annoying rats and roaches), and homes with swimming pools (the horror!).

SUNBLOCKED

In 2012 Violet and Zoe Michener came home after a school Field Day with such severe sunburns that their mom rushed them to the hospital. Why didn't they just put on sunblock? Because according to the FDA, it's an "over the counter drug." Only one state (California) allows kids to apply sunscreen at school without a doctor's note.

HUGGING BAN

Everybody needs a good hug—except…not if you go to school in New Jersey. Afer what he called some "incidents of unsuitable, physical interactions," Matawan-Aberdeen Middle School Principal Tyler Blackmore announced to students that they were now in a "no hugging school." Offenses noted at this school and others include female field-hockey players hugging after winning a big playoff and a 14-year-old boy hugging his female best friend. Meanwhile, 19 states still allow public school teachers to spank students. (Ouch!)

FACE FADS

And you thought faceBOOK was the weirdest face fad.

- Ever wonder why the subject for Leonardo da Vinci's *Mona Lisa* thought the no-eyebrow look was a good one? Apparently it was all the rage in Europe in the early 1500s. A completely hairless face was considered a sign of beauty. Women plucked their eyebrows, eyelashes, and even their hairlines.

- Eighteenth-century Europeans used to shave off their eyebrows and glue on fake ones made from…mouse skin. Mouse-skin brows were thought to be more beautiful and luxurious than natural ones. To make the mouse-brow falsies, first you (or—more likely—your servant) had to catch a mouse, skin it, clean the skin, and then cut out eyebrow-shaped pieces. Then you used glue made from fish skin and bones to stick them on. Believe it or not, this fashion statement was a sign of wealth. People would adjust their fake eyebrows in public or place them faraway from the natural brow to call attention to the fact that they were wealthy enough to have mouse-skin brows stuck to their faces.

- Men from the Mentawaian tribe in Indonesia believe pointy teeth make women more attractive. So female tribe members get to look forward to tooth sharpening in their teens. The procedure is simple: a village leader hits a wooden brick against a metal chisel and carefully breaks off tooth pieces until the young woman's teeth look something like vampire fangs. No medications are used to mask the pain, and the women heal their mouths by sucking on green bananas. (Fangs a lot!)

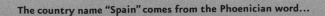

POTATO SURPRISE

You don't need superpowers to do this experiment.
Super-physics will do the trick.

WHAT YOU NEED:

- 3 straight drinking straws
- 3 raw baking potatoes
- an audience

WHAT TO DO:

1. Give two audience members a potato and a straw. Tell them that whoever gets the straw farthest into the potato without bending the straw wins.

2. After about 15 seconds, hold the fatter end of your potato in your non-writing hand. Keep your hand and fingers away from where you want the straw to go in and come out of the potato.

3. With your writing hand, grab the straw and cover the top of the straw with your thumb. With a quick motion, stab through the narrower end of the potato with your straw and say, "I win!"

HOW IT WORKS:

The edge of the end of the straw is sharp and thin like a knife. By capping the end of the straw with your thumb, you trap the air inside and compress the air molecules. That creates air pressure within the straw that keeps it more rigid than it was without the air pressure. With air pressue inside it, the straw becomes strong enough to go right through the potato.

...**"ispanihad," which means—"the land of rabbits."**

THE DOCTOR IS "IN"-SANE

Home remedies have been a medical staple throughout human history, but that doesn't make them any less questionable.

RUN WHILE YOU CAN

Having trouble "going" or "going" too much? There's a folk-remedy "cure" for that. For the "flux"—better known as "the runs"—drink a tea brewed from sheep dung and eat a dried, pulverized chicken gizzard. For constipation, brew tea from bark taken from the *east* side of a peach tree. Or...chuggalug the blood of a dying rooster.

WART'S THAT?

According to one folk remedy, warts will disappear if you rub bacon on them—but only if the bacon has been buried under a rock first. Another remedy requires rubbing the wart with a bean and then throwing the bean into a well. If those remedies fail, visit a cemetery and rub the wart three times over a tombstone.

BETTER WET THAN...

Folk remedies to "cure" bedwetting may be worse than a few soggy mornings. The first isn't so bad: put a bucket of water beneath the bed. The second? Put head lice on a piece of bread and eat it. The third remedy? Pee into an open grave (and risk arrest...or worse still, haunting). All three of these folk remedies must be performed under the light of a full moon to have any chance of success.

THE HORROR...

Q: How can you write dozens of Goosebumps books without being more than a little weird and spooky? A: You can't.

HOW I GOT MY SHRUNKEN HEAD

"I was a weird kid," says author R. L. Stine. "I was not social at all. I found this old typewriter in the attic. I dragged it down to my room and started typing little magazines, like *Tales to Drive You Batty*. My mother was always saying, 'Go outside and play! What's the matter with you?'"

Stine's still spending his days inside, writing at his desk. He shares his home office with a three-foot-long cockroach, but don't worry—it's not alive. It's a papier-mâché prop from a play based on one of his stories. His purpose in life is "to terrify kids," and he's good at it. How good? Stine has written more than 300 scary books. His Goosebumps series alone has sold more than 300 million copies worldwide, and he's the second-most best-selling children's author of all time (behind Harry Potter author J. K. Rowling). So how does one writer come up with so many creepy ideas? Well, he certainly doesn't do research. In fact, he says, "Almost everything comes from my twisted imagination."

REVENGE OF THE LAWN GNOMES

"My major talent is thinking of good book titles," Stine says. "One day, I was in a bookstore and these words just popped into my head: 'Say Cheese and Die.' Where did that come from? I have no idea! But it's a great title."

After the title comes the "what if" stage? "What if these boys

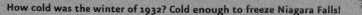

find an evil camera?" "What if they start taking pictures with it, and the camera takes pictures in the future of bad things that happen." Stine's titles lead to questions and those questions lead to books. And sometimes...his books lead to problems with the "book police"—parents and other people who think R. L. Stine's writing is too creepy for kids.

YOU CAN'T SCARE ME!

Stine doesn't agree. "Kids are very smart," he says. "They know the difference between real violence and fantasy violence." In an interview with the *Village Voice*, he said even more: "People who go after violent things for kids just don't like kids. If there's something kids really like, people will find something bad about it. If there's a hairstyle kids like, the school bans it. Any music? It's trash. It's horrible."

R. L. Stine's Goosebumps books made the top-twenty list of most-challenged books between 1990 and 1999. "Both charges seem rather ridiculous with titles like *Go Eat Worms!, The Cuckoo Clock of Doom*, and *It Came from Beneath the Sink*," writes PEN America blogger Alissa Nutting. Nutting thinks the popular Goosebumps series and its spin-offs "respect children enough to confirm what they already know: The world is not always safe."

As for R. L. Stine, even though he spends so much of his time thinking about spooky stuff, he claims it doesn't affect him. "I never get scared," he says. "I don't know what the feeling is. Horror always makes me laugh." (*Bwa-ha-ha!*)

Did You Know? *The three subheads in this article are titles of books in R. L. Stine's Goosebumps series.*

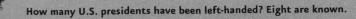

How many U.S. presidents have been left-handed? Eight are known.

THESEUS AND THE MINOTAUR

When the gods interfere, weird things happen.

It all started when the sea god Poseiden sent a handsome white bull to Queen Pasiphae of Crete. Shortly thereafter the queen—who was married to King Minos—gave birth to a monstrous creature that was half man and half bull. The king wasn't just displeased, he was embarrassed. So he hid the monster—they called him the Minotaur—in a labyrinth beneath his palace in Knossos. This maze was designed to be so complicated no one could find a way out. Most of the time, King Minos ignored the Minotaur. But when the beast got hungry, its bellows shook the palace and no one could get a good night's sleep. The king's solution? Send a prisoner or two for the Minotaur to snack on.

One year, the king's son Androgeus headed to Athens to compete in the Panathenaic Games (sort of like today's Olympics, but with chariot races and naked athletes). Androgeus didn't win the games. In fact, he was killed by the same bull that had fathered the Minotaur. King Minos was furious! He told Aegeus, king of Athens, that he would send a boat with black sails to Athens. King Aegeus was to put seven of the city's young men and women on that boat and send them back to Crete...or else!

In Thailand, polo players ride elephants, not horses.

Every nine years, fourteen young Athenians boarded the black-sailed ships, never to return. They were either enslaved to wealthy families or sent into the labyrinth to be killed—and eaten—by the Minotaur. After about twenty years of this, Theseus, son of Aegeus, was sick of the slaughter. "I shall volunteer as tribute!" the prince announced. He would go to Crete as one of the seven young men. But he did not intend to be eaten. He planned to kill the Minotaur and end the human sacrifices once and for all.

"Don't worry, Dad," he told his father, the king. "I'll be back. When you see the ship returning with white sails instead of black, you will know that your son lives and the Minotaur is dead."

When Theseus showed up in Crete, King Minos rubbed his hands together. At last, his own son's death would be avenged. And if Theseus managed to kill the Minotaur? All the better! He'd be rid of a major embarrassment and Theseus would be stuck in the labyrinth...until he died. Things did not go as Minos imagined. That night, a lavish last supper was served to the tributes. King Minos's daughter, Princess Ariadne, attended the feast. She spotted the handsome young prince across the room. Instead of weeping and wailing like the other thirteen tributes, Theseus was eating and drinking and telling jokes. Ariadne found him too yummy for words. Before the evening ended, the two royal youngsters had fallen madly in love.

The princess went to the man who had built the labyrinth and pleaded for his help. He gave her a magic ball of golden thread for Theseus to carry into the labyrinth. When he entered the maze, the prince put the ball on the ground. It unrolled and unrolled, twisting and turning as it led him toward a dark chamber filled with brittle bones and reeking with the smell of death: the Minotaur's lair! The prince battled the Minotaur, got him in a headlock, pounded his head against the floor, and killed him. Then he followed the magic thread out of the labyrinth and into the princess's arms. (Swoon!)

Did all end well? Not exactly. Dionysus—the god of wine— came to Theseus in a dream and told him not to marry Ariadne. So he dumped her on an island on his way back to Athens. In all the hoopla, he forgot to change the boat's sails from black to white before he reached home. When King Aegeus saw the black sails, he went nuts. He was sure that his son had died a horrible death and that it was his fault for letting him go to Crete. "My son, my son!" he wailed, and then he threw himself from a cliff into the sea.

That is how Theseus became King of Athens (Thanks, Dad!) and also, so the myth says, how the Aegean Sea got its name.

*   *   *

SMELL YA LATER!

During the 1300s, deadly plagues killed nearly 50 percent of Europe's population. Real doctors fled the cities, and untrained "plague doctors" stepped in to treat patients. Plague doctors wore special suits to protect themselves: long black high-necked coats; leather pants; wide-brimmed hats; and "bird masks." The masks had red-glass openings for the eyes (to protect the "doctor" from evil) and elongated beaks filled with sweet-smelling herbs (to protect them from the "bad air" believed to be causing the plagues).

Found in Australia: fossils of a 10-foot-tall giant kangaroo.

DEVILISH WEATHER

*Check out how these naturally occurring "devils" spin
their way around our world...and beyond.*

WATER DEVILS

Imagine you're out on a boat in a warm ocean—it's completely
calm with just a few clouds in the sky. You spot a light-colored disk
forming on top of the water. The disk is surrounded by a darker
area. Pretty soon, the dark and light areas begin to spiral together.
The spiral swirls, throwing off sea spray. As it whirls upward, a
column of water rises from the surface high into the air and begins
to spin wildly. Sailors call these spinning towers "water devils;"
scientists call them "waterspouts." These watery devils occur
when warm humid water heats the cooler air above it. That makes
the air unstable. The humid air above the ocean contains a lot of
water vapor, and the clash of hot and cold turns that vapor into a
towering tornado-like vortex. By the way, if you DO spot one of
these things, don't sit in your boat watching it. Get out of its way
and seek a safe harbor.

DUST DEVILS

If you're out in a desert on a clear day, you may have seen a
column of dust swirl up from the ground. The dusty vortex usually
dances around harmlessly and lasts less than a minute. That's a
"dust devil" and it happens because of hot rising air. When hot

Official language of the United States? There isn't one!

air coming off the ground meets cooler air above, the varying pressures can lead to spinning winds. Since dust doesn't weigh much, it lifts off the ground and spins around like a dirt tornado, but it's not very strong and therefore isn't destructive like a tornado. A bit of rain is all it takes to keep Earth's dust devils down. But these dusty whirlwinds don't just happen on Earth—they have also been documented on Mars. On Mars they last a lot longer. Because of low air pressure and low temperatures, there is no rain on Mars. Martian dust devils can last for months!

FIRE DEVILS

Like dust devils, "fire devils" rise from the ground rather than coming down from the clouds. Sometimes called *fire whirls* or *firenadoes*, fire devils are rarely witnessed by human eyes. Why? Because they happen in the middle of blazing wildfires when a superhot spot of ground sends up a plume of heated air. "They start to rise very rapidly," New York state's climatologist Mark Wysocki told *LiveScience*. "As things start to rise, they suck the surrounding air in like a vacuum. Then you get this twisting that begins to resemble a vortex." Fire devils grow long and skinny, like ropes of fire. They can extend as high as 100 feet into the air (tall as a 10-story building) and spin at up to 100 miles per hour.

Devilish Fact: With more than 400 water devils per year, the Florida Keys holds the record as water-devil central. More waterspouts happen there than anywhere else in the world.

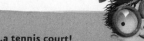

The first computer was as long as...a tennis court!

HOP, SKIP, JUMP!

*Kids all over the world have been jumping rope for
hundreds of years. No wonder they're so tired!*

JUMP LIKE AN EGYPTIAN

Ancient Egyptians and Australian Aboriginal people were some of
the first to pick up the sport. Since they didn't have rope, they used
thin bamboo or wild vines instead. Experts think jumping rope
was mainly a training exercise for hunters who needed to outrun
threatening animals or warriors hoping to beat others in combat.

DON'T BURST A VESSEL

In the early 1800s, jump rope became a kids' game. Even girls—
considered delicate back then—were allowed to play...as long
as they exercised caution. In *The Girls' Own Book*, author Lydia
Maria Child wrote: "I have known instances of blood vessels burst
by young ladies," she wrote. "In a silly attempt to jump a certain
number of hundred times, [they] have persevered in jumping after
their strength was exhausted."

ROPIN' RECORDS

Some girls ignore the Lydia Childs of the world. In 2012 Japanese
skipper Jun Tanizawa set a Guinness World Record on live TV for
the most double dutch jumps in one minute (221). Competitive
rope skipper Jolien Kempeneer of Belgium set a slightly more
unusual record in 2010 when she pulled off 100 jumps in 30
seconds in the "single-rope, right-foot-only" competition.
Neither Jun nor Jolien burst any blood vessels.

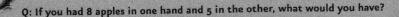

Q: If you had 8 apples in one hand and 5 in the other, what would you have?

QUACKY HEADS

Some fashionable practices should never be revisited.

THE CHONMAGE: Buzzed in the front and top of the head with some leftover hair pulled into a ponytail or bun in the back, This special hairdo was the ideal cut for Japanese samurais in the seventeenth and eighteenth centuries. Why? It helped them keep their helmets securely on their heads while in battle.

THE COMMODE: At the end of the seventeenth century, French and English women wore gaudy head-toppers called *fontanges* (in France) or *commodes* (in England). A typical commode had several tiers and towered a foot high. The complicated headpieces were made of lace, silk, and gauze. Heavy wire frames gave them shape, ensured that the fabric tiers stood upright, and (most likely) were a huge pain in the neck.

THE MULLET: Hair cut short in the front and left long in the back didn't start in America in the 1980s or even with the 1994 Beastie Boys hip-hop hit *Mullet Head*. Historians say the cut goes all the way back to Neanderthal times. Cave-dwelling humanoids probably just wanted to cut a bit of hair out of their eyes. Ancient Egyptians, however, turned the mullet into a fashion statement. Egyptian mullets were wigs made of black wool or flax. Women—as well as men—wore them. With the rise of the Roman Empire, mullets went out of favor. Long hair was considered "barbaric," and the mullet was banned in the Roman military. Why? Because long locks in the back made it easy for an enemy to grab a soldier's hair, pull back his head, and cut his throat.

A: Really big hands!

LOVE IN VEIN

Time for a nap? Some of the best ideas have come to people while they slept.

IN YOUR DREAMS

In 2003 Stephenie Meyer was in what she calls "zombie mom" mode. She'd been married for 15 years and had three young sons. "They didn't sleep; they all had colic and ear infections endlessly, and so I just didn't sleep for six years. I was always tired, and I always had a crying baby on me somewhere. My whole life was about basic survival. About keeping them breathing and fed." On June 2 of that year—Meyer remembers the date because it was the first day of her sons' swim lessons—she went from "zombie mom" to "vampire writer," and it all began...with a dream.

"I woke up from a very vivid dream," Meyer writes on her website. "In my dream, two people were having an intense conversation in a meadow in the woods. One of these people was just your average girl. The other person was fantastically beautiful, sparkly, and a vampire. They were discussing the difficulties inherent in the facts that a) they were falling in love with each other and b) the vampire was particularly attracted to the scent of her blood and was having a difficult time restraining himself from killing her immediately."

FORK OVER THE CASH

Meyer had a million mom things to do that morning—making breakfast for her hungry children, getting them dressed, searching for swim trunks—but she couldn't stop thinking about the dream.

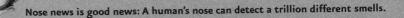

Nose news is good news: A human's nose can detect a trillion different smells.

Of course, eventually she got out of bed and took her kids to swim lessons. But afterward, Meyer—who had never written a book in her life—sat down at the computer to write down her dream before it faded. "Short-term memory loss is one of the hazards of motherhood," Meyers said in a *Cynsations* blog interview. Meyers wrote ten pages that first day. Three months and 500 pages later, she had the first draft of a novel titled *Forks.* Never heard of it? No surprise. The editor whose company paid $750,000 for the right to publish the book changed the title to *Twilight.*

FANGS FOR THE RESCUE

Twilight and its sequels have millions of fans. The books have sold more than 100 million copies worldwide. They've been turned into movies, and the young actors cast in the main roles of Edward and Bella (the couple from the dream) have been catapulted to stardom. But the book that came from an exhausted mom's dream has plenty of critics as well. Bella has been described as a "droopy, drippy character" who is so clumsy and hapless that her vampire boyfriend has to constantly come to her rescue.

So why does Meyer think the girl in her dream (and in the book) couldn't resist the sparkly boy who could barely keep from sinking his fangs into her? And why can't fans resist her books? "Vampires," Meyer says, "have a dual nature. They are frightening and deadly, but they are also alluring. They have attributes we envy, such as eternal youth. They are often attractive, rich, powerful, and educated. They sometimes wear tuxes and live in castles. The paradox there makes them hard to resist, at least…as subjects for stories."

Eek! About 200 new computer viruses show up every month.

MORE AMAZING KIDS

On page 128 we told you about three super-talented kid athletes. Meet six more athletes who found fame before adulthood.

Rock-climber Brooke Raboutou was only a year old when she first started scaling walls. She's won titles as an elementary school student, where she is recognized for her ability to quickly scale steep natural rock walls. Brooke's mom, a professional rock climber, is her coach. Before every climb, Brooke and her mom make a "pinkie promise" to be good to each other all day. In 2012, at age 11, Brooke became the youngest person to climb a 5.14b route. In climbing speak, that means "extremely challenging" and only for expert climbers. Even though she's been competing for six years, Brooke still gets butterflies. That's why she always wears two lucky scrunchies—one black with multi-colored stripes and one red with flames—when she competes.

Soccer prodigy Leonel Angel Coira from Argentina was 7 years old when the professional fútbol team Real Madrid recognized him for his amazing footwork skills. Real Madrid signed Leonel to a yearlong contract to train with their youth team. At age 9, he's still going strong. "My dream is to play in the first division with Madrid and for Argentina in the World Cup," he said.

Q: How long does it take a chipmunk to store food for the winter?

Slugger Ariel Antigua from New Jersey was just 5 years old when he amazed his family, friends, and strangers by sending 90 mph fastballs right back at the pitcher who threw them. That batting skill is common for professional players, but for a little kid? It's nothing short of astounding. "The day he picked up the bat, it's like he knew what to do with it," his father said. "You'd throw the ball and he'd hit 98 of 100 when he was less than two." Major League teams are already watching over Ariel, but for now, he's just having fun playing baseball with his friends.

Football running back Demias Jimerson from Arkansas was such a standout star in his league that officials decided to invent a rule to prevent him from scoring another touchdown if he had already done so three times in one game. Without the rule, Demias dominated every game he played in. Demias wasn't too upset. Why not? The rule only applied to his sixth-grade season…after that, he'd be free to score as many touchdowns as he could.

Hockey player Oliver Wahlstrom from Maine first got recognized for his wicked-good scoring skills when he was 9 years old. When Oliver played on a team with kids much older than him, he would score more than 150 goals in just 40 games. He's known for complicated and tricky methods of scoring—like spinning around on the ice. At age 13, Wahlstrom was recruited to play for the University of Maine's Black Bears. He's still too young to sign an official "letter of intent," but Oliver has already made a verbal commitment to join the Bears. Not bad for a middle school kid!

*　　*　　*

A: Only two days!

BIRDLANDIA

Match these real U.S. towns with their states.

1. Byrdstown
2. Chicken
3. Bird-in-Hand
4. Goose Pimple Junction
5. Eagleville
6. Pigeon Forge
7. Turkey Scratch
8. Parrotsville
9. Birdseye
10. Parrot
11. Buzzard Roost

A. Arkansas
B. Tennessee
C. Mississippi
D. Pennsylvania
E. Missouri
F. Virginia
G. Indiana
H. Alaska
I. Kentucky

Hint: Three of these bird towns are in the same state.

Answers on page 286.

Seriously? There's a town in Denmark named Middelfart.

REALLY COOL ROBOTS

Want a robot that brings you tacos? How about one you can control with your mind? As it turns out, the future is here....

The Robot: Rapiro, Rapiro Company, 2013
What's It Do? It's a foot-tall humanoid robot that you can program to make a cup of coffee, manage your computer calendar, tell you the weather, and even dust your bookshelf. Bonus: It never asks for a holiday.

The Robot: TacoCopter, Skycatch Company, 2011
What's It Do? Say good-bye to your friendly neighborhood delivery guy. In the near future, when you have the munchies, you'll go online, place an order, and then wait for the TacoCopter—a flying robot with a carrying case for food—to deliver it to your doorstep. (Slight setback: Due to federal flight restrictions, the TacoCopter is only allowed to do demonstrations right now.)

The Robot: Humanoid Kinect robot, Disney, 2012
What's It Do? Disney Research's robot is one of the first electronic creations that's capable of physical interaction. It has a cupped "hand" that it uses to catch colored balls thrown by a human partner, and it's even able to throw balls back to the partner and keep a juggling pattern going. When the robot misses a catch, it looks down and shrugs or shakes its "head."

BOMB-SNIFFING WHAT?

You've probably heard of bomb-sniffing dogs, but these bomb finders just might blow you away!

OH, RATS!

After twenty years of civil war, Mozambique, Africa, is riddled with land mines. They're buried just below the ground and triggered to explode when stepped on. About twenty people step on these mines every month. The result? Blindness, loss of limbs, even death. The United Nations calls them "an insidious and persistent danger" to children. And, once planted, land mines can remain active for up to 50 years.

More than 100,843 land mines have already been cleared from northern Mozambique. But there are at least another 520 minefields left in the central and southern parts of the country. Bomb-detection dogs can sniff out land mines, but if a dog steps on a mine, it might be heavy enough to trigger an explosion and... good-bye dog. An international mine-clearance group called APOPO decided to find a lighter-weight animal to train. The animal they chose had bad eyesight, but since you can't see a mine buried underground, that didn't matter. It was supersmart, which made it easy to train. And—best of all—it had a great sense of smell. What was it? The African giant pouched rat.

African giant pouched rats are about three times bigger than ordinary rats. They grow to be about the size of a house cat and

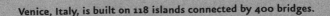

can be trained to recognize the chemical scent of an explosive, just like bomb-sniffing dogs. After about nine months of training, the rats are loaded into cages and trucked to an area suspected of being mined during the war. They set to work, wearing small harnesses attached to ropes that stretch between two human handlers on either sides of a field. If a rat smells an explosive, it scratches the ground over the land mine. While human helpers defuse the mine, the rat gets a treat: Bananas are a favorite.

When APOPO brought in the first batch of trained rats in 2006, locals were skeptical. "In Mozambique we eat rats," joked Alberto Augusto, director of Mozambique's national demining institute. "It was very strange to see them working and demining. We were thinking to grill them." The rats soon changed Augusto's mind. They're superfast at clearing mines. An area that would take a human team with a metal detector two weeks to clear can be cleared by rats in a single day. By 2014 trained rats had found 2,700 land mines in Mozambique. "They're doing a great job," Augusto told *Discovery News*.

*　　*　　*

"Dear Math, please grow up and solve your own problems. I'm tired of solving them for you."

—**Anonymous**

"I have not failed. I have just found ten thousand ways that won't work."

—**Thomas Edison**

What happens if you tickle a gorilla? It laughs. (We're not joking!)

WHICH WAY TO CANADA?

No compass, road map, or GPS required. Not for these super navigators of the animal world.

THE GREAT NAVIGATION MYSTERY

Canadian geese fly thousands of miles between western Canada and Mexico without getting lost, but how do they find their way? Do they remember the shapes of the mountains and rivers? Do they use the stars and the sun or have an internal compass? Wish we could tell you, but scientists don't really know. Here's what they do know: Geese fly day and night at speeds of up to 45 miles per hour. They have superstrong necks and wings and can fly over 12,000-foot mountain peaks. As for that "V" formation? It helps reduce air resistance. Each goose flies just in front and slightly above the next bird, providing a bit of a wind shield. That shield makes flying easier and conserves energy for those long-distance goose commutes. The geese take turns being front man on the "V". When the bird in front tires out, it drops back to let the next goose in line take over.

ANIMAL MAGNETISM

They're not the smartest animals in the sea, but Caribbean spiny lobsters get a gold medal for their navigational skills. Using Earth's magnetic fields, they use a built-in compass to pinpoint their exact location. Researchers at the University of North Carolina tried to trick the lobsters by moving them to a test site about 23 miles away, but the plucky crustaceans found their way home.

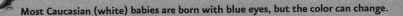

Most Caucasian (white) babies are born with blue eyes, but the color can change.

TURTLE POWER

On August 10, 1996, a loggerhead sea turtle named Adelita took off from Baja California into the vast Pacific. Like all female sea turtles, Adelita was heading to the beach where she was hatched to lay her own eggs. In her case, that beach lay off the coast of Japan, about 9,000 miles from Baja. Adelita had spent most of her life in captivity. Could she find her way home? Before releasing her into the Pacific, marine biologist Wallace J. Nichols attached a transmitter to Adelita's shell. He tracked her journey across the Pacific via satellite. It took 368 days—just over a year—but Adelita made it home. How? Using an internal compass that lets her perceive Earth's magnetic fields. "Just like we sense gravity and know which way is up or down, a sea turtle senses 'home'," says Dr. Nichols.

THE GREAT POOP AXIS

Ever wonder why your dog circles around and around and sniffs the ground before pooping? Scientists at the Czech University of Life Sciences in Prague have the answer. After watching 70 dogs do their business for two years (that's about 1,893 poops), they (the humans) discovered that the dogs always pooped in a north-south axis. So, besides those 200 million sensors in their noses, dogs use the earth's magnetic fields. Why a north-south axis? Yet another mystery of the animal world waiting to be solved.

For more amazing animal navigators, go to page 220.

*　　*　　*

BIOHACK U

*Live forever? Learn to fly? Start your car with a wave of your
hand? In the near future, you might be able to do
just that...if you're willing to biohack yourself.*

BIOWHAT?

In the computer world, hackers are computer geeks
who break into other people's computing systems,
sometimes just for fun and sometimes to cause
trouble or even steal things. That's why hacking is
illegal. Biohackers don't hack computers; they hack
their own bodies. Why? They're looking for ways to
upgrade their bodies using technology. "We hack
our bodies with artifacts from the future-present,"
states one biohacking website. Good idea? Well,
Dr. Anthony Guiseppe-Elie, professor of bioengineering at the
University of South Carolina says, "Anyone doing this should
stop!" Here are a few biohackers who didn't.

THE TECH: Southpaw, designed by electronic engineer and
biohacker Brian McEvoy, is a miniature compass to be implanted
under your skin.

WHAT IT DOES: An ultrathin whisker sticks out of Southpaw's
rounded titanium shell. When you face north, the whisker tickles
the underside of your skin. "It would be best located near the
shoulder," says McEvoy, who plans to be the guinea pig for testing
his own device.

THE TECH: Internal earphones, invented by 34-year-old salesman and biohacker Rich Lee

WHAT IT DOES: When Rich Lee woke up one morning nearly blind in one eye, he decided he'd better improve his hearing to make up for losing his sight. How? By implanting gold-coated sound-transmitting magnets in the *tragus* of each ear. What's a tragus? We're glad you asked. It's that hard protrusion at the front of the ear opening. Lee wears a wire coil around his neck that converts sounds into electromagnetic fields. Those fields turn the magnets into "internal headphones." With a media player, amplifier, and battery pack hidden under his shirt, Lee can listen to music all day long with no one the wiser. He can also "hear" heat from a distance and detect magnetic fields and Wi-Fi signals.

THE TECH: Xnt implantable NFC (Near Field Communication) chip, sold by biohacking firm Dangerous Things

WHAT IT DOES: Have you seen the chip that gets taken out of Jason Bourne's hip in *The Bourne Identity*? How about the one that's injected into Katniss Everdeen's arm in *The Hunger Games*? Then you know just what this thing looks like. The Xnt chip gets implanted into your hand between your thumb and index finger. Once it's there, the chip emits a low-power radio-frequency signature that can "trigger pre-programmed events." In layman's terms, that means it can open locks, start a car, and unlock a computer or smartphone. All you have to do is wave your hand at the lock or device. But first…you have to either inject it into your hand or find someone else who's willing to do so. (Good luck with that!)

*   *   *

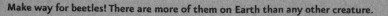

Make way for beetles! There are more of them on Earth than any other creature.

WORST MOVIE SEQUELS OF THE MILLENNIUM

If one is good, more must be better, right? Well...no.

TRON: Legacy (2010)

IT FOLLOWS: *TRON* (1982)

IT'S ABOUT: A son who looks for his missing father and is pulled into the virtual world his dad designed

WHY IT STINKS: When the original *TRON* was released, special effects weren't that advanced, so the moviemakers decided to go bananas with the sequel. The film's $170 million budget (most of it for special effects) earned the honor of being the most money ever spent by a first-time director. Shooting the movie took 64 days. Post-production effects took 68 *weeks*. So...the movie looks cool, but the story defies logic. As one *We Got This Covered* reviewer said, "Leave your brain at home."

Dumb & Dumberer: When Harry Met Lloyd (2003)

IT FOLLOWS: *Dumb & Dumber* (1994)

IT'S ABOUT: The high school days of the movie's star idiots, Harry and Lloyd

WHY IT STINKS: *Dumb & Dumberer* took Harry and Lloyd about 10 years back in time, and neither of the original actors (Jim Carrey and Jeff Daniels) returned to play their parts. Without the comic stars that made the first movie work, the sequel is an unfunny rip-

Did you know? The world's smallest insect, the fairyfly...

off. "Words fail to express my dismay at having wasted a half hour of my life on this film," wrote one reviewer. It's also set in the 1980s. Nuff said?

Legally Blonde 2: Red, White & Blonde (2003)

IT FOLLOWS: *Legally Blonde* (2001)

IT'S ABOUT: Law school graduate Elle Woods, who heads to the nation's capitol to protest animal testing

WHY IT STINKS: Ditzy but smart Elle Woods (Reese Witherspoon) made the first "Legally Blonde" movie a success. But even she couldn't do much with the Capitol Hill setting, which is known for putting schoolchildren to sleep in U.S. History classes across the country. The sequel also lacks the humor that the original had. As *Entertainment Weekly* put it, "Making things pink is not a substitute for jokes."

Ace Ventura: Pet Detective Jr. (2009)

IT FOLLOWS: *Ace Ventura: Pet Detective* (1994) and *Ace Ventura: When Nature Calls* (1995)

IT'S ABOUT: The son of kooky detective Ace Ventura, who has to bail out his mom when she is wrongfully arrested for panda theft

WHY IT STINKS: The movie went straight to TV, which is a dead giveaway that even the producers knew it was horrible. Ace had no son in the previous films and wasn't even married, so setting up a sequel with a character that never existed and none of the original cast was a recipe for disaster. One reviewer noted that the film "should come with a health warning" and offered a helpful bit of advice: "If you see this film in the bargain bins at your local video store, buy every copy you can, take them outside, stamp them into tiny pieces, and then burn the crumbs."

...is too small and weak to fly. Fairyflies have to let the wind carry them!

D'OH KIDDING!

*Being a fan means wearing a hat in the shape of a wedge
of cheese to a Packers' game. Being a FANATICAL fan?
That requires more effort.*

BART INVADES NYC APARTMENT

The Simpsons debuted in 1989, and in its 26 seasons on the air
has broadcast 559 episodes (so far), making it the longest-running
American sitcom ever. What would it take for a fan to impress
Homer, Marge, Lisa, Bart, and even Maggie Simpson? How about
packing a 10-by-10-foot room in your New York City apartment
with Simpsons memorabilia? That's what 30-year-old Jeremy
Wilcox has done. Wilcox's *Simpsons* collection, the largest in New
York City, includes more than a thousand toys and posters.

Morgan Spurlock, the documentary-maker who filmed *Super
Size Me* also directed *The Simpsons 20th Anniversary Special: In
3-D! On Ice!* Spurlock interviewed Wilcox and featured his room
for the special. "At times I wondered if this is a normal hobby for
a thirty-year-old to have," says Wilcox. "But to be featured in the
special? It was worth it."

WHAT'S THAT SMELL?

In 2012 FOX TV hosted a *Simpsons* marathon to promote the
show's 500th episode. The winners? Two California students:
Jeremiah Franco and Carin Shreve. In the process of winning,
they broke the Guinness World Record for the longest stretch of
continuous television viewing—86 hours and 37 minutes—over
three and a half days without sleep. The winners got a whopping

big check for $10,500. As for the losers? Shreve says something (or someone) started to smell so horrible it was hard not to puke. And the guy stting next to her? He totally lost it. "He started asking stuff like 'What's up with the car that we're in?'" Shreve's response: "Uh, dude? We're not in a car. We're sitting on a couch."

MR. TOMACCO

Rob Baur, a senior operations analyst at an Oregon sewage-treatment company, grew a real life "tomacco," a mix of tobacco and tomato plants based on *Simpsons* episode 231, "E-I-E-I D'oh." In the show, Homer becomes a farmer and grows what he hopes will be a mega-cash crop: tomatoes that taste horrible but are as addictive as cigarettes. In the show, Bart eats a tomacco and then spits it out, saying, "That's horrible! I want another one!"

Baur, who earned the name "Mr. Tomacco," grew the real deal by grafting a tobacco root onto a tomato stem. He's a big-time *Simpsons* fan, but his reason for growing the tomacco was much bigger. *The Simpsons* episode used humor to show what happens when tobacco companies think more about profit than people. Both of Baur's parents smoked; both got cancer from smoking. His dad lost a lung. His mom lost her life. As for the tomacco? It gave Baur a tiny bit of payback for those tragic losses.

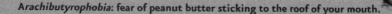

Arachibutyrophobia: **fear of peanut butter sticking to the roof of your mouth.**

DR. QUACK

Have a pain? Why not get someone to stick you where it hurts with a pointed metal rod? Yeah…that's what we think, too.

IT'S ELECTRIC!

In 1795 Elisha Perkins was a respected Connecticut doctor and the president of the local medical society. By all accounts, he was good at his job…at least until he made what he believed to be a major scientific breakthrough. Perkins's breakthrough? He had "discovered" the source of all physical pain. Perkins claimed that the scientific reason for pain was…"noxious electrical fluid." Nasty electrically charged fluid built up in the human body. The cure? Perkins had discovered that, too: drain the fluid and—*ta-da!*—no more pain.

Metal conducts electricity. Maybe that's why Perkins decided that to remove or "extract" the bad electrical fluid, he should stick the affected body part with a piece of metal. Afterward, he would wave the piece of metal over the patient for a few minutes to draw the negative energy out into the air where it would be harmless to the patient. In 1796 Perkins filed a patent for his invention. He honestly believed the thing worked, and he also believed it would make him very rich. He called his pain-removal device the "Perkins Patent Tractors."

Does the idea of a leech on your leg horrify you?

HEAVY METAL

Perkins loved to demonstrate his tractors on willing patients. The device consisted of two three-inch-long steel-and-brass rods. One end of each rod was flat and the other end was pointy. Though made of commonly found metals of the day, Perkins claimed that the mixture of the two metals created a fantastic new alloy that had "profound scientific powers." What kind of powers? Perkins's Patent Tractors could supposedly cure almost every common medical complaint of the day. Headaches? Cured! Arthritis? Cured. Gout (a painful swelling of the toes or feet)? Cured! Facial pain? Cured. Stomachaches? You get the idea.

Perkins's Patent Tractors became a sensation in the U.S. and England, where Perkins's son reportedly sold $50,000 worth of the things. Back home in Connecticut, Perkins's medical colleagues were not impressed. Though he'd been the president of his local medical society before obtaining his patent, in 1797 its members called him a quack and kicked him out.

ACCIDENTAL IMPACT

Perkins died in 1799, but that wasn't the end of the story. In fact, medical historians now point to Perkins and his Tractors as important to the development of modern medicine. (Huh?) Seeking to prove that Perkins's Tractors were quackery, Dr. John Haygarth of England's Royal Society conducted what we now call a "clinical trial" for the device. Haygarth tested the Tractors in a controlled environment to see if they really worked. And—surprise! Based on the responses of test subjects, they seemed to do what Perkins had claimed. In case after case, patients said they had "immediate relief" of pain after being treated with the Tractors. What they didn't know? Haygarth wasn't always treating them with Perkins's device. He treated some test subjects with "fake" tractors made of wood. Haygarth's conclusion: The trials "clearly prove the wonderful effects the passions of hope and faith, excited by mere imagination, can produce upon diseases." Today doctors call this "the placebo effect." And placebos—harmless pills, medicines, or procedures—play a major role in the development and testing of new drugs and treatments. (Thanks, Dr. Quack!)

*　　*　　*

ACCUSTOMED TO YOUR FACE

Famous chefs' faces are often plastered on cookbook covers and food products, but celebrity chef Rachel Ray was blown away at a New York book signing when she saw her face tattooed on the back of a fan's right shoulder. Chef Andrew Zimmern had a similar experience. Though the chef many call simply "AZ" has no problem chowing down on gross-out foods such as sautéed crickets, porcupine, and jerk pig's head on his Travel Channel show, *Bizzare Foods,* seeing his face tattooed on the leg of Ohio tattoo-artist Ben Hatfield must have been a bit stomach-turning. AZ had just one question for his biggest fan: "Why?"

EPIC MAKEOVERS

How far would you go to prove you're a fan?
These folks went all the way to Cloud Cuckoo Land.

FAN: Mikki Jay, a mother of three from Britain

HOW FAR? Jay has spent over $16,000 on plastic surgery (two nose jobs, a chin implant, and cheek implants) to make her look like the late entertainer, Michael Jackson. "When Michael released his *Bad* album in 1987, people started saying I looked like him," says Jay. In 1991 she entered a talent contest impersonating Jackson, and won. Since then, she's appeared in front of royalty and performed live as Michael Jackson in "The Legends of Rock" and "Rock Stars of Today." Though surgery is expensive, Jay has no regrets. She claims to make $240,000 a year impersonating "The King of Pop." But her biggest thrill came at a London show celebrating the 20th anniversary of Jackson's album *Thriller* when she met the singer backstage. "It was one of the proudest moments of my life," Jay says. "He sang along with me and blew me a kiss."

FAN: 33-year-old New Yorker, Justin Jedlica

HOW FAR? Jedlica has reportedly spent over $150,000 on more than 140 procedures in his quest to look like "Ken," the boyfriend of Mattel's Barbie doll. "I've operated on nearly everything that's possible to operate on, and I've customized my body from head to toe, but I still want more." Jedlica's "pride and joy"? His shoulders. "Nobody has anything like them," he claims. "I'm working with a silicone-fabrication company to do an artistic muscle-augmentation-implant line." (Whatever that means...)

WEIRD WILLS

Death demands don't get much quackier than these.

THE DECEASED: S. Sanborn, hatmaker

THE WILL: Donating one's body to science? Fairly normal. Asking an anatomy professor to use the skin from your body to make two drums? Not so normal. Leaving the drums to a friend and asking the friend to take the drums to Bunker Hill once a year at dawn and use them to play "Yankee Doodle"? Quacky enough to make it into this Bathroom Reader.

THE DECEASED: Marvel Comics editor Mark Gruenwald

THE WILL: After he died, Gruenwald wanted to be immortalized in a Marvel comic. Most people might think that meant writing him in as a character, but no—Gruenwald's will requested that his cremated ashes be made into ink used to draw a comic. "He wanted to be part of his work in a very real sense," said Marvel's editor-in-chief. In 1997 Gruenwald got his wish with a limited-edition reprint of "Squadron Supreme," which he had co-authored several years before.

THE DECEASED: John Bowman, a Vermont millionaire

THE WILL: Bowman's wife and two young daughters all preceded him in death. He was convinced that after he died, they would all be resurrected together. His request? He wanted servants to prepare dinner for four every night and leave it out in the dining room of his mansion so his family could devour it upon their return. (Hey, ghosts get hungry, too!)

Egg test: A fresh egg will sink in water. A rotten egg will float.

BLOODY STRANGE

When you think of blood, unless you're picturing space aliens, you're probably seeing red. We'd like to change that.

- One drop of blood contains millions of red blood cells. Mammals have a component called *hemoglobin* in their blood. Hemoglobin—which carries oxygen around the bloodstream and removes waste—has a lot of iron in it, and iron gives blood its red color. Without red blood cells, your body would slowly die.

- Lobsters, crabs, snails, spiders, and octopi all have blue blood. Why? Because they don't have hemoglobin in their blood; they have *hemocyanin*. Hemocyanin is made up of copper instead of iron, and copper absorbs all colors except blue.

- Many insects and invertebrates, for example, houseflies and Marine worms, have green blood. This is caused by *hemolymph*, a watery fluid that lacks red blood cells but still transports nutrients throughout the body. Hemolymph contains *hemocyanin* in addition to other pigments, which causes the greenish blood color. When houseflies are killed, the red liquid left behind is just pigment from their eyes, not red blood.

- Other animals like Samkos bush frogs and Green Tree Skinks (a kind of lizard) also have green blood, but for a different reason. The green pigment *biliverdin* is a waste product that is typically processed in the liver. But these frog and lizard systems pass biliverdin back through their blood instead, causing it to be green.

For more colorful blood, turn to page 210.

Russia's giant Siberian tiger weighs up to 600 lbs.

HOLIDAYS YOU NEVER HEARD OF

Proof that the U.S. isn't the only country that knows how to party!

STRAW BEAR DAY

Where: Whittlesea, England

When: Second weekend in January

Background: In the 1800s, Straw Bear Day was celebrated annually in small villages across the eastern half of England. On Plough Monday (the first Monday after January 6 in the Christian calendar), a man or boy would be covered with straw until he was virtually unrecognizable and couldn't even see. Village people would lead the "straw bear" from house to house, and he would dance at each stop. In exchange for this little display, villagers gave him money, food, or beer. The celebration marked the first day farmers put their shoulders to the plough after the Twelve Days of Christmas.

Party On! Straw Bear Day died out in the early twentieth century, but Whittlesea residents decided to resurrect it in 1980. They kept the tradition of covering a man in straw from head to foot, but they now leave eye openings and have him dance in public places rather

than at private residences. Fearing that a hay-covered man isn't quite as entertaining in the twenty-first century as in the nineteenth, they hire clog dancers and musicians to perform with him.

BEAN-THROWING FESTIVAL

Where: Japan

When: February 3 or 4

Background: *Setsubun* (Bean-Throwing Day) marks the beginning of springtime. It was originally considered to be a new year's celebration. Why throw beans? *Mame-maki*, the bean-throwing ritual, is meant to vanquish the previous year's evil so bean-throwers can start the new year with a clean slate.

Party On! To prepare for the big party, bean throwers roast a pan of soybeans. Then they fill a cup with the beans, crack open a few windows, and toss the beans, yelling "*Oni wa soto! Fuku wa uchi!*" ("Out with the goblins! In with fortune!") To add to the fun, a family member sometimes dresses as a goblin so everyone else can hurl beans at the "evil spirit."

MONKEY BUFFET FESTIVAL

Where: Lopburi, Thailand

When: Last Sunday in November

Background: Thai people living in Lopburi wanted to boost tourism, and they knew they could do it by making people aware of the special animals in their town. In 1989 a local hotel manager devised the Monkey Buffet Festival as a way of yelling "Hey! Look at our monkeys!" Officially, the holiday is meant to honor Hanuman, the Hindu monkey god.

Party On! Lopburi has more than 3,000 long-tailed macaques, and local chefs draw them out for a day of celebration by preparing a massive feast. The city shells out more than $15,000 every year to create and lay out 4,000 pounds of food for the monkeys. Offerings include fruit, sausage, ice cream, and cans of soda (which the macaques pick up and drink just as you would). Locals and tourists must stay in marked areas to watch the monkeys pig out.

BABY-JUMPING FESTIVAL

Where: Castrillo de Murcia, Spain

When: The Feast of Corpus Christi (usually in June)

Background: This Catholic holiday dates back to 1620 or 1621. Like most Catholic celebrations, it's all about the triumph of good over evil. In many ways, the festival is like a baptism—intended to drive out what the Church calls "original sin" and put newborn babies on the path to happy, successful lives.

Party On! The key part of this festival is the baby-jumping, known as *El Colacho*. Residents put mattresses in the town square and lay any babies born within the last year on the mattresses. A local man dressed in a bright-yellow devil costume then takes a flying leap and jumps over all of the babies. Although no one has ever been injured in the festival (according to its organizers), the Pope discourages Spanish priests from being involved in the risky ritual.

ROUKETOPOLEMOS

Where: Vrontados, the Greek island of Chios

When: Midnight prior to Easter Sunday

Background: No one seems to know how *Rouketpolemos*

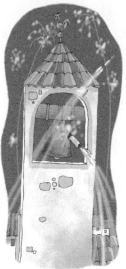

(literally Rocket War) originated, but locals have been celebrating it for a long time. Some say local sailors once used their ships' cannons to defend the island against pirates. Later, locals started firing the cannons on Easter, for heaven knows what reason. In the 1800s, rival churches on opposite ends of town—St. Mark's and Panagia Erithiani—decided a rocket war made the perfect Easter kick-off (though they now mark the holiday with homemade explosives instead of cannon fire).

Party On! Before the first shot is fired, rival church "gangs" prepare around 25,000 homemade rockets. A few days before Easter, they board up both churches' windows and doors. Then they wrap the churches with wire sheeting. Why? To protect worshippers who will be celebrating midnight mass inside while rockets burst overhead. When the services begin, so does the rocket war. Each church fires a series of rockets aimed to hit (and ring) the bell in the other church's bell tower. Whichever church lands more direct hits wins, but here's the catch—no one ever manages an exact tally (they're probably too busy running for cover), so, when morning dawns, the churches vow to do it all again next year.

As you can imagine, this little bash takes quite the toll on the town of Vrontados, where residents have to board up their windows and doors. "We can't breathe when it takes place," said one local. "We have to be on standby in case a fire breaks out, because if you are not careful you can even lose your house."

...on La Reunion Island in the Indian Ocean (east of Madagascar).

GO OUT & PLAY

But not until you've read about these wacky new sports!

HASH IT OUT

Around 1837, British schoolboys had fun and stayed fit with a game called "Hares and Hounds." Some players (called "hounds") chased others (called "hares") across fields, hedges, streams, bogs, and hills. The helpful hares left scraps of paper for the hounds to follow. By 1867 adult Englishmen had decided "paper chasing" each other around London was a good way to keep fit.

Fast forward to 1938: A group of bored Englishmen living in Kuala Lumpur (a city in what is now Malaysia) decided to restart the chase. They called their group the Hash House Harriers because they started each run from the Selangor Club where some of them lived and ate. Seems the club's food was bad enough to be called "hash." They met every Monday night for a "Hares and Hounds" chase and ended each run with food and drink at the club.

It took a while, but hashing has caught on in a big way. Today, there are now 3,000 hash clubs in 200 countries. Most hashers are adults who end their runs with a pint or two at a favorite pub. But some "hash houses" now have junior and family runs. The hare still sets out first to mark a trail with paper, chalk, or flour. Runners follow. Whistles or horns help runners stay together, and the encouraging call of "On-On!" eggs on stragglers. Hashers chase through all kinds of terrain: city streets, maze-like suburbs, dusty

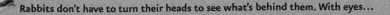

Rabbits don't have to turn their heads to see what's behind them. With eyes...

deserts, soupy swamps, even through storm drains. And there's always a party at the end of the trail.

A GORGE-EOUS WALK

In the U.S., some families think a hike from the car to the mall is enough exercise for a weekend. In the U.K.? Family fun sometimes includes gorge walking. If that doesn't sound much tougher, here's a clue: Gear for a gorge walk includes a helmet, a wetsuit, a life jacket, waterproof boots, climbing equipment, and throw lines. That's because a gorge walk isn't just a hike on a trail along the edge of a spectacular gorge. Gorge walkers scale down steep rockfaces to the bottom of river gorges, then they "walk" the river…no matter what kind of wild terrain it leads through. Sliding down water-slick rocks, churning through rapids, jumping between boulders, diving over waterfalls…any of these adrenline-pumping activities can (and probably will) happen on a gorge walk. Most of the adventure happens in Wales and Scotland, where impressive rock formations offer some of the best gorge walks on the planet.

CATCH THE WAVE

Thousands of years ago, ancient Egyptians surfed on planks made of wood and pottery. But not on ocean waves. They surfed waves made of sand: dunes as much as 500 feet high. The rest of the world didn't catch the sand wave until the 1970s, about the same time snowboarding started. Sandboarding lagged behind until the invention of slick formica boards revved up dune-riding speeds enough to attract daredevils. Now, it's worldwide: Germany hosts the world sandboarding championships, Egypt offers rides on the Great Sand Sea (72,000 square kilometers of dunes—the biggest

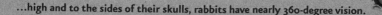

...high and to the sides of their skulls, rabbits have nearly 360-degree vision.

dune field on Earth), China boasts the Desert of Death (a place where people go in but don't come out), and the U.S. has the 40-mile-long Oregon Dunes Recreational Park. Sand's up!

WHAT THE ZORB?

Every kid knows how much fun it is to tumble down a grassy hillside. And who hasn't bounced a ball down a slope? But combining the two? It took the manufacturing imagination of a New Zealand company to combine a giant hamster ball with rolling down a hillside and turn it into an extreme sport. It's called *zorbing*, and the sport took off around 1996.

How does zorbing work? First, you climb inside a gigantic inflatable ball about 10 feet in diameter. Once you're inside the ZORB (we prefer the term Human Hamster Ball), you get pushed down a hillside. Pretty soon you're careening along at about 30 miles an hour. The ZORB is actually two clear balls in one: the outer ball is supposed to act as a shock absorber to cushion the bumps down the hill while the zorber rides safely inside the inner ball.

How safely? Even if riding on a course approved for safety by the company that invented the balls, this is an extreme sport. And on unapproved courses…the sport can be deadly. In 2013 a 33-year-old Russian man died when the ball he and a buddy were rolling in left a ski slope and flew into a gorge. "There were no shouts or screams," said the buddy who survived. "Just fear—as I looked into Denis's eyes for the last time before everything went black." New Zealand inventor ZORB Limited said the men were not on an approved course or using one of their ZORB balls.

No contest: a cockroach can hold its breath for 40 minutes.

DUMB SELFIES

"Selfie" may be 2013's official Word of the Year, but before you hold up a cell phone and take a picture of your face, please...engage your brain.

- In 2013, two Swedish teens stormed into a burger joint wearing black ski masks over their faces and brandishing a 12-inch knife. Frightened workers handed over $400 cash, and the girls made a run for it. Forty-seven minutes later, police arrested the thieves and confiscated a smartphone. On it? A selfie taken before the robbery. The girls thought their robbery gear and honking big knife would make a great selfie. Not so much... but it did make convicting them of robbery easy.

- A teen got his friends to gang up on a 16-year-old boy so he could steal the other boy's Samsung Galaxy Epic smartphone. Then he snapped a selfie with the stolen phone. What he didn't know? The phone was set to automatically e-mail all photos to its owner. Police identified the thief using the selfie he'd unknowingly e-mailed to his victim.

- A 21-year-old Spanish man climbed on top of an electrified train to take a selfie. For some reason he assumed that because the train was stopped, the high-voltage wire atop it would not be electrified. Wrong: 3,500 volts of electricity shot through his body, instantly killing him.

- A private in the U.S. Army posted a photo of herself hiding in her car to avoid saluting the American flag. Bad move. She's facing investigation and could spend two years in prison.

Pounds of avocados eaten during Super Bowl XLVII? 79 million.

MORE QUACKY JOBS

*Here are a few more jobs to answer the question posed
on page 118: "Why get stuck in a boring job?"*

FAKE GORE MAKER

Audiences at Washington, D.C.'s Atlantic Theater should have
known they'd be in for some stomach-churning action before they
took their seats. After all, "The Lieutenant of Inishmore"—a play
by Martin McDonagh—is about an Irish terrorist with a taste for
cruelty. But the audience might not have been prepared for the
carnage created by assistant stage manager and gore expert, Freda
Farrell. We're talking severed limbs, dead animals, and gallons of
fake blood splattered on the stage. Getting it to look real is no easy
task, says Farrell. "There are actually nine different mixtures of blood
in the play." Her biggest challenge? To come up with a "recipe" that
freaks out the audience but is easy to clean up between scenes. For
the goriest scenes, Farrell used a mixture of peanut butter, chocolate
syrup, Karo syrup, water, and red and blue food dyes. (Yum!)

SWORD MAKERS

Even if the blood looks real, a play can flounder if the fight scenes
seem fake. Casey Kaleba, who directed *Romeo and Juliet* for the
Folger Theater in Washington, D.C., wanted his fight scenes
to "feel" and "sound" dangerous." So he hired Kerry Stagmer
and his brother, Matthew, of Baltimore Knife and Sword. The
brothers make custom-made steel weapons for festivals, theater

productions, and video game companies. Although they usually spend one to two years on each order, they had less than a week to make three pairs of swords for *Romeo and Juliet*. Want to buy a set of your own? It'll cost you $2,500.

WILD FUNGUS HUNTERS

Ever hear of Chemult, Oregon? Unless you're a wild-mushroom expert, probably not. Once a year, this town of 135 in south central Oregon morphs into the hub of the wild matsutake mushroom trade. For two months each fall, southeast Asian-American families descend on the area. They comb through the woods to hunt for the "mastsi" or set up tents to buy them. Although picking wild mushrooms in the Oregon woods sounds kind of cool, today it's a tough way to make a living. Back in the 1990s, a pound of mushrooms went for $600. Today, you're lucky to get $5 bucks.

VERMIN EXTERMINATOR

Michael Jones has seen more than his share of creepy crawlies. As the owner of Hawkeye Exterminating in Waterloo, Iowa, Jones cleans out carpenter ants, termites, and cockroaches from homes and office buildings. "Roaches are hands down the worst," says Jones. Once he got a call from a woman whose walls, floors, and ceilings were crawling with roaches. "They were falling on our heads, there were so many," he says. "It's a dirty job, but someone's got to do it."

*   *   *

In Tokyo, Japan, dogs can take private yoga lessons. Cost? $34 a session.

TOTALLY TUBULAR QUIZ

Parents tell you they were cool in the 80's? Give them this test to see how they really rate: Lame? Or totally tubular?

1. Book
   a. a true fact
   b. a rule that's super annoying to follow
   c. to get out of a place really fast

2. Butter's
   a. a person who's always making lame excuses
   b. something nice
   c. someone who tells lies all the time

3. Cheeuh!
   a. a tasty snack
   b. saying that something's obvious
   c. a way to tell someone to get lost

4. Chonies
   a. underwear
   b. bedrooms covered in horse posters
   c. the "cool kids"

5. Crunchy
   a. permed hair
   b. something that's gross
   c. feeling jealous

6. Dip
   a. a nerdy person
   b. an in-ground swimming pool
   c. to interrupt a private conversation

7. Exo Skeleton
   a. excellent
   b. clothes

How many of America's top five most-polluted cities are in Calfornia? All five.

c. braces

8. Grindage

    a. a hard week at work (or school)

    b. food

    c. dancing to punk rock

9. Homefry

    a. a pizza delivery

    b. a note sent home from school

    c. best friend

10. Kirk Out

    a. to get really upset over something

    b. to hang up the phone

without saying goodbye

    c. to act like you're the boss

11. Scoshe

    a. an uncool car

    b. a bookworm

    c. a little bit, not a lot

12. Swirly

    a. dunking someone's head in the toilet and flushing

    b. a gigantic moustache

    c. twirling an index finger in the air (to show you think something's crazy)

Answers on page 286.

*   *   *

THOSE AWESOME 80s

Music: Michael Jackson, Madonna, Dire Straits, Prince

Movies: *The Breakfast Club, Sixteen Candles, Pretty in Pink, E.T., The Goonies,*

Toys: Cabbage Patch Kids, My Little Pony, Rubik's Cube

ETC: Sony Walkman, Hair Bands, The Clapper, Wrestlemania, The Legend of Zelda, Frogger

Tubby tabby? Fifty-eight percent of American cats are overweight.

BLOODY STRANGE (PART II)

On page 197, we told you that red-blooded doesn't apply to all creatures on Earth. Here are more bloody-weird facts.

- Mackerel icefish live off the coast of Antarctica in deep water. These fish have no red blood cells or hemoglobin. Instead, they have a clear "anti-freeze" type of blood that prevents ice crystals from forming inside their bodies.

- When ladybugs feel threatened by predators, they try to defend themselves by "reflex bleeding." This means that the ladybugs will release a yellow-orange blood from their leg joints. The liquid smells so bad that animals learn to back off.

- The blood of alligators and crocodiles has been shown to be much better at fighting infections such as HIV and MRSA than human blood. Why? Antimicrobial peptides—protein fragments—in their blood boosts the reptiles' immunity to infections. Scientists are working to create medications from alligator and crocodile blood proteins.

- Some drugs can change the color of a human's blood. They bind to hemoglobin and change the chemistry of the iron atom, causing the blood to change color. A sulphur-containing migraine treatment called *sumatriptan* can actually make a patient's blood turn green.

If a turkey looks up during a rainstorm, it might drown.

EXOTIC PETS

When it comes to pets, some people just won't settle for "normal."

- In the 1920s, a famous dancer named Josephine Baker liked to take her pet cheetah to the cinema in Paris. When the movie ended, they'd run outside and leap into a waiting Rolls Royce.

- In 2003 magicians Siegfried and Roy were on stage in Las Vegas with a white tiger. Halfway through the show, the tiger grabbed Roy by the neck and dragged him offstage. Roy lost 25 percent of his skull, but…he lived.

- Pop star Rihanna had an adorable little fuzzy bug-eyed animal on her neck in September 2013 when she tweeted a photo of herself on tour in Thailand. Just one problem: The animal was a loris and it's a protected species. Police tracked down a 20-year-old man and a 16-year-old boy who'd been using the loris to get tips from photo-happy tourists like Rihanna, and rescued the animal.

- In 2013 pop star Justin Bieber had his capuchin monkey, Mally, seized by authorities at the airport in Munich, Germany. Seems Bieber sneaked Mally into Germany aboard his private jet. After spending time in quarantine, Mally joined other monkeys at Serengeti Park in Hodenhagen. His Bieber-less new home is a tree-covered island zoo workers have dubbed "Mally-bu."

Kid quote: "What happens at Grandma's stays at Grandma's!"

BIRD-BRAINED

It doesn't just mean "annoyingly stupid" anymore.

BIRD: Alex, an African Grey Parrot

GIFT: The name "Alex" wasn't picked at random. It stood for Avian Learning Experiment. That's because Alex spent most of his life under the watchful eye of Dr. Irene Pepperberg, a psychologist at Brandeis University and Harvard. Pepperberg bought the bird in 1977 from a pet store. At the time, scientists were still debating whether or not other animals could learn to communicate with humans. Within a short time, Dr. Pepperberg had Alex doing just that. Though he had a brain about the size of a walnut, the bird acted as intelligent as a kindergartner. He recognized colors and shapes. He could count. He had a 150-word vocabulary and even picked up common phrases like "calm down" and "good morning" from hanging out in the science lab where he was studied. Alex also knew how to communicate emotions. When Alex was moved into a new cage, he told his trainer, "I want to go back." Alex lived to be 31 years old. His last words: "You be good. I love you."

BIRD: Snowball, a Medium Sulphur-Crested Cockatoo

GIFT: Snowball loves to dance to music by bobbing his head, stomping his feet, and shaking his body to the beat. The talented bird has a series of Youtube videos, which have racked up more than 15 million total views. One of his most popular performances is a dance to the song "Another One Bites the Dust" by Queen. Although there are other animals that hear and move to musical melodies, biologists who have studied Snowball believe that he's the first animal to truly rock to the rhythmic patterns of music.

The only animal that makes food humans can eat: bees.

BIRD: Einstein, an African Grey Parrot
GIFT: Einstein spends her days at the Knoxville Zoo scaring visitors with her evil laugh and amazing them with her 200-word vocabulary. If you stop by to say hello to her, Einstein might respond with a flirty "Hey, sweetheart." She also does some spot-on animal impersonations. She can crow like a rooster, bark like a dog bark, oink like a pig, meow like a cat, and impersonate a chimpanzee's squeaky call. Most fun of all? Einstein can sing "Happy Birthday" on cue.

BIRD: Poll, an African Grey Parrot
GIFT: In June 1845, friends and family of President Andrew Jackson (the guy whose face is on the $20 bill) gathered for his funeral. Just as the service began, a African Grey Parrot named Poll started squawking out...curse words. The Reverend William Menefee Norment shared the story of Jackson's profane parrot in Samuel G. Heiskell's *Andrew Jackson and Early Tennessee History*: "Before the sermon and while the crowd was gathering, a wicked parrot that was a household pet got excited and commenced swearing so loud and long as to disturb the people and had to be carried from the house." Poll was the president's pet. Perhaps he was overcome by emotion at the thought of his owner's death. It's believed that Poll learned how to curse from the president but that didn't stop the other attendees at the funeral from being shocked by the parrot's foul language and bad behavior.

*　　*　　*

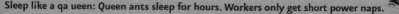

Sleep like a qa ueen: Queen ants sleep for hours. Workers only get short power naps.

NO WEIGH TO TRAVEL

Think turbulence or lost luggage is the worst thing that can happen when you travel? Read on!

WEIGHT A MINUTE!

Step up to the ticket counter at any airline and you'll be asked to put your luggage on a scale. Seems fair. After all, there's that whole thrust-to-weight ratio pilots have to consider to make sure they can get their planes off the ground. But a Southwest Airlines employee thought luggage might not be the only overweight thing on a 2011 Easter Sunday flight out of Dallas. The agent reportedly "eyeballed" passenger Kenlie Tiggeman and her mother and then told them that they were…too fat to fly.

Seems Southwest actually has an official "Customers of Size" policy. If a passenger can't fit in the 17-inch space between armrests, they should "proactively purchase" the needed number of extra seats prior to travel. Apparently Tiggeman and her mom hadn't been proactive. During the "Customers of Size" discussion, the gate agent actually asked her weight and clothing size…in front of other passengers. Big no-no! Southwest policy says such conversations should happen in private. In a last-minute attempt at a save, the agent said the mom and daughter could fly if they sat in the row with another overweight woman.

A Southwest rep showed up at the gate and apologized to Tiggeman for the embarrassment. The carrier refunded her fare and offered both women free travel vouchers, which they accepted.

The airline might have hoped that would be the end of it. What they didn't know: Tiggeman is a weight-loss blogger. The story of Southwest's treatment of overweight travelers soon went viral.

THE POOP CRUISE

In February 2013, the Carnival Triumph cruise ship left Galveston, Texas, for a four-day pleasure cruise to Cozumel, Mexico, with 4,200 people on board. Three days into the trip, fire broke out in the machine room. The good news: the crew put out the fire. The bad news: the power, sewage, heating, and air-conditioning systems were no longer working. And the ship was adrift off the coast of the Yucatán Peninsula in the Gulf of Mexico.

According to passengers, things went from bad to truly disgusting. There was no air conditioning, so interior cabins turned into sweltering saunas. Taps didn't run, so there was no way to bathe. Food and drinking water were soon in short supply. Guests ate mustard sandwiches and small slivers of ham. Most looked out for themselves, and some hoarded food. It was "like the Hunger Games," said a 24-year-old passenger from Houston, Texas.

Worst of all—the toilets no longer flushed. Before long, the cruise ship's bathrooms and hallways were flooded with human waste. Passengers were handed red biohazard bags and told to use those and stay out of the overflowing toilets. Some refused. "People were doing crazy things and going to the bathroom in sinks and showers," said 30-year-old Jason Combs.

After five days adrift, tug boats towed the cruise ship from off the coast of Mexico to Mobile, Alabama. Think that was the end? Nope. Passengers had to be bussed home. One bus broke down… at 2:30 a.m.…stranding passengers on the roadside.

COUNTRY MYTHS

Here's what some folks believe...down on the farm.

- Kill an ant or disturb an anthill, and there's a price: rainy weather will follow.

- If ants travel in a straight line, it's going to rain. It's also supposed to rain if the ants are running around in circles. (Hmm...) And if they show up at the doorstep early in the week? Expect showers by Sunday.

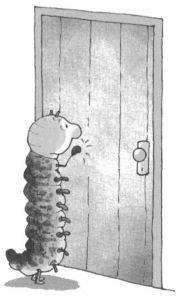

- If a caterpillar crawls up to the door in August or September and tries to come in, get ready for a cold winter. If it changes its mind and goes away, the season will be mild.

- Large spiders invading the house all summer long? Look for a harsh winter.

- When the first bumblebee comes buzzing at the door, spring has arrived.

- Large numbers of lightning bugs in June foretell a hot summer.

- If flies start dropping from the ceiling? Not only will you have flies in your hair, you'll know that summer weather is over and fall will arrive soon.

Female lions hunt together. They stalk prey in open areas under cover of darkness.

BIRD WORDS

*Sure, most of these are clichés, but that just makes it easier
to fill in the blanks with the missing bird-related words.*

1. Like water off a _____ back

2. That doctor is nothing but a _____.

3. A _____'s eye view of Parrotsville

4. Don't get your _____ up!

5. _____ of a _____ flock together.

6. He _____-ed her on.

7. The early_____ catches the worm.

8. Do not let the _____ of sorrow build a nest on your head.

9. Get your _____ in a row.

10. Never tell secrets to a stool _____.

11. Please stop _____-dogging me!

12. Blind as a _____

13. I'm finer than a box of _____.

14. Don't be a _____brain.

15. Gramps is no spring _____.

16. Don't spend your _____ egg.

17. A wild _____ chase

WORDPLAY

Just for fun, substitute
sandwich, frog, raisin, mouse,
or *porcupine* in each blank.

Answers on page 286.

DOCS GONE WRONG

Don't let these stories make you afraid of going to the doctor or dentist. Just let them show you how important it is to choose one who's not psychotic.

INITIAL SHOCK

Carving your initials into a school desk, tree, or wet slab of cement? Bad...but not awful. Carving them into a patient's body during surgery? Beyond awful. While performing a Caesarian section on a pregnant woman, Dr. Allan Zarkin was apparently so pleased with his surgical skills that he used a scalpel to carve his initials above the incision. His patient, Liana Gedz, was not impressed. "I feel like a branded animal," she said at a news conference.

Zarkin's excuse? According to his lawyer, the surgeon suffers from a brain disease, similar to Alzheimer's, and should not be held responsible for his behavior. The jury disagreed. Zarkin was sentenced for assault, had his medical license revoked, was fined $14,000, and is facing a lawsuit that will likely cost him an even bigger bundle. Gedz wants to carve a hole in his bank account to the tune of $5.5 million.

DISAPPEARING TEETH

When 21-year-old Christopher Crist went into Amazing Family Dental he was in a lot of pain. He'd decided to have three teeth pulled. That seemed like a lot, but it would be worth it to be pain-free. The dentist gave him some pills to ease the pain of oral surgery. "The pills made me loopy," Crist told reporters. So loopy that he didn't realize that the dentist hadn't stopped at three teeth: he'd pulled 32—every tooth in Crist's mouth. According to other reports, this is not the first time a patient had walked out of Amazing Dental with far fewer teeth than when they walked in. The sign on the door of the practice might offer a clue. It reads "Natural Dentures: Making your new smile true to life." Christopher Crist isn't smiling—he's suing.

BACK IN FIVE

Everybody's entitled to a break once in a while, but patient Charles Algeri certainly didn't expect Dr. David Arndt to take one in the middle of performing spinal surgery. During the operation, Dr. Arndt repeatedly asked the nurses to find out if his paycheck had arrived. When another surgeon stopped by to drop the check off, Arndt asked him to watch his patient for "about five minutes."

Arndt walked out of the hospital, got behind the wheel of his car, and drove to his bank to cash the check. Why? He needed money to fund his raging methamphetamine habit. Five minutes turned into more than half an hour, and when Algeri found out what had happened, he sued the surgeon for malpractice. Dr. Arndt's insurance company had to fork over a $1.25 million settlement. At last report, Arndt was finishing up the 12-year prison sentence for abandoning his patient during surgery.

*　　*　　*

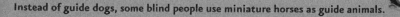
Instead of guide dogs, some blind people use miniature horses as guide animals.

HARD TO LOSE

On page 184, we told you about some of the world's best animal navigators. If you thought those were amazing, wait till you read about these!

THE EAR KNOWS

After hanging out in the ocean most of their lives, adult sockeye salmon leave the ocean and return to the head of the streams where they were born. Like sea turtles (see page 185), they make the trek to lay their eggs, and they use a built-in compass that can sense the earth's magnetic fields. But, like dogs, salmon also sniff their way home. As for how they know to swim upstream? According to fish ecologist Simon Thorroid, a bone in their inner ear called an "otolith" guides the way. The salmon's otolith shows the fish which way is up just as the fluid-filled network of canals and chambers within the human ear help us tell up from down.

LOST IN FLORIDA

When their 4-year-old tortoiseshell cat, Holly, went missing in Daytona Beach, Jacob and Bonnie Richter figured they'd lost her for good. Two months later, Holly turned up in West Palm Beach about a mile from home. Two hundred miles of Florida coastline separate the two seaside towns. So how did Holly find her way home? Neuroscientist Matthijs van der Meer credits the cat's "visual memory." Her main clue: the ocean. "She may have remembered which side the ocean was on during her northward journey," said van der Meer. "But it may have been a lucky guess."

FOLLOW THE LEADER

They're practically blind, but somehow ants travel huge distances in search of food. For a long time, scientists thought that ants use their antennae to follow a chemical trail left by other ants. They do…at least on the first trip to a certain location. But further study produced a new discovery: After making a journey once along a chem trail, ants can actually remember specific geographical landmarks and use them to travel back and forth between food and nests.

* * *

BARBIE VS. MRS. POTATO HEAD

What do you want to be when you grow up? Kids get asked this question a lot. Two researchers wanted to find out if a popular toy might influence a kid's choice. Which toy? Barbie! Girls were given three toys to play with: a Barbie dressed like a model, a Barbie dressed like a doctor, and a Mrs. Potato Head. After playtime, the researchers gave the girls a list of 11 possible occupations. Girls who had played with the Barbie dolls (both the model doll and the doctor doll) chose more traditional female careers, such as teacher, librarian, or flight attendant. Girls who played with Mrs. Potato Head? They chose firefighter, pilot, or police officer more often. Who knew a potato could have so much influence!

DEATH MYTHS

Are these folk beliefs about death and dying true? You decide.

- A clock stopping at either noon or midnight warns of an impending death.

- Never have two ticking clocks in the same room—that will bring death to the household.

- Carrying an ax or a hoe into the house brings death within the year. And if a brick tumbles off a house's chimney, death will visit. (Sooner rather than later if it lands on your head.)

- A wild bird flying into a house or a dog howling three times under a window are both considered death omens.

- Keeping the coins used to cover a corpse's eyes brings good luck. But spend them quickly or bad luck will follow.

- Coffins should always be carried out the door feet first. Why? If they're not, the spirit might "look back" into the house and choose someone for the Grim Reaper to take next.

- Seeing a white chicken while on the way to a funeral is considered bad luck. White horses? Those are bad luck, too. If a white horse is allowed to follow a hearse, then another death will happen in the family.

- Don't want to be haunted by the person who just died? Pee on the new grave three mornings in a row. (*Please note: Uncle John does not endorse peeing on graves, so don't blame him if you do it and get caught.*)

- To make sure a spirit "moves on," pay the funeral bill right away. A spirit cannot rest until the bill's been paid.

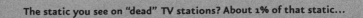

The static you see on "dead" TV stations? About 1% of that static...

ODD ANIMALS

These critters take the definition of "odd duck" to a new level.

GOT LEGS?

Though smaller than a pinky finger, the half-inch long *Illacme plenipes*—the acme of plentiful legs—claims the title "leggiest creature on Earth." Government scientists discovered the burrowing insect in 1926 but thought they'd gone extinct. The next one wasn't spotted until 2005, when University of Arizona entomologist Paul Merek found one on a foggy hill near San Francisco. What does it take to win the "leggiest creature" award? Seven hundred and fifty legs. As if that wasn't weird enough, this millipede has claws at the ends of its legs for digging and can make its own "clothes." How? It spins silk from long hairs that cover its back.

HOW RUDE!

Planning a trip to Borneo? Better stay clear of an adorable bug-eyed primate called the Slow Loris. It's small and furry with raccoon-like eye patches, and it will cling sweetly to your arm with its long furry fingers. But don't  be fooled. When threatened, this nocturnal primate rubs its hands in a dark fluid released from a gland above its elbow. It mixes the gunk with its own saliva, rubs the goo on its teeth, and bites whatever is bugging it. Its bite injects a flesh-rotting poison into its victim, which can be fatal to humans. The shift from cuddly to deadly leads to the Slow Loris's nickname: jungle gremlin.

...is leftover radiation from the Big Bang that began the universe.

PANDABAT

Researchers DeeAnn Reeder and Adrian Garside spied a black bat with creamy-yellow spots and stripes while working in the South Sudan in 2013. Bizarrely, the bat's patterning looked a lot like a panda's. They'd stumbled upon "the find of a lifetime" and they knew it. Back home in the United States, Reeder and her colleagues in the biology department of Bucknell University determined that the panda-patterned bat was so unique, it qualified for its very own genus: *Niumbaha superba*. "Niumbaha" means "rare" or "unusual" in Zande, the language of the bat's Sudanese neighbors.

GOING (MORE THAN) THE DISTANCE

In January 2013, one female pigeon flying in what should have been a 600-mile race in Japan took a wrong turn and ended up in… Canada! The pigeon's 5,000-mile detour took it all the way across the Pacific to Vancouver Island in Western Canada. Exhausted and scrawny, the tough bird managed to survive its ordeal. At last report, a Canadian racing club planned to adopt the world traveler and breed her to create "a 'good stock' of future racing pigeons."

THINK PINK

What animal oddity did Charles Darwin miss when he visited the Galapagos Islands in 1835? The pink iguana! Not surprising, since the pink iguana lives only on the Wolf volcano at the northern end of Isabella Island, an area Darwin did not explore. Fast-forward to 2009: that's the year scientists officially recognized the pink iguana as a unique species—*Conolophus marthae*. "What's surprising is that a new species of megafauna, like a large lizard,

If a dolphin is sick, other dolphins will push it to the surface so it can breathe.

may still be found in a well-studied archipelago," reported *National Geographic News*. Typically, iguanas are yellow or green. So why's this rare breed salmon-pink? Nobody knows. And with only about 100 of the creatures in existence, scientists worry that the species will go extinct before they have time to figure it out.

THINK PINKER

It's slimy. It's eight inches long. It's hot pink. And it lives in only one place on Earth: the peak of Mt. Kaputar in New South Wales, Australia. Locals call the creature the "giant pink slug," but its official name is *Triboniophorus aff. graeffei*. How pink is it? "As bright pink as you can imagine," says Michael Murphy, a ranger with the Australian National Parks and Wildlife Service. Scientists say the hot pink color acts as camouflage. That doesn't make a lot of sense unless you know that the giant pink slug naps the day away under eucalyptus trees. Fallen eucalyptus leaves are red, and the pink slug can stay well-hidden from predators nestled among them. When they do emerge, the bright pink slugs really show their stuff. "On a good morning, you can walk around and see hundreds of them," says Ranger Murphy.

WHAT BIG EYES...

What has eight legs and eyes the size of basketballs and weighs as much as a whale? The giant squid, the biggest invertebrate on Earth. Until recently, few scientists had seen a live one up close. For one thing, they live 3,000 feet below sea level, a dangerous depth for deep-sea divers. They're also pretty shy. "They're huge. They're weird-looking," says Leslie Schwerin, director/producer of *Monster Squid*, whose crew captured rare footage of the squid for the Discovery Channel. "But they're just gentle giants."

Gobble, gobble! **More turkeys are raised in California than in any other state.**

STUPIDER APPS

If you thought the apps on page 147 were dumb...

APP: Crazy Mouth
DESCRIPTION: Transform yourself into a living cartoon character. Select one of the 10 fully animated mouths, hold your iPhone or iPad up to your face, and turn yourself into the most annoying kid at the party.

APP: iFart
DESCRIPTION: I fart, you fart, we all fart—on demand—with this app. Choose from 20 gross farting sounds, including Silent but Deadly and Burrito Maximo. Don't spare your friends: the Social Fart Icon lets you share the iFart experience with friends. Just post a pic of that burrito you ate for lunch and choose "Burrito Maximo" from the fart wheel. Your Facebook followers can listen to butt music right on their smartphones.

APP: Fake-An-Excuse
DESCRIPTION: Need an excuse to break loose? Fake-An-Excuse has been loaded with more than 45 realistic sounds to make it easy to get you off the phone. Put the call on speakerphone, hit the iPhone's Home button, load the Fake-An-Excuse

Earth's core temperature is estimated to be between 7,000°F and 12,000°F.

app, and select the excuse sound effects you want to play during the call. Excuses include, "Bees! They are everywhere," "A riot is about to break out," and "I need to go to the bathroom."

APP: iBacon
DESCRIPTION: Mmmm... bacon. "Cook" four pieces of bacon on a skillet, flip them when they look ready, drain the fat, and then "eat" the bacon (talk about a low-fat diet!). Caution: If you use the automatic video loop, you'll have to deal with emergencies such as grease splatters and a blaring smoke alarm.

APP: Type n Walk
DESCRIPTION: We all know it's dangerous to text and drive. But some of us are so klutzy we can't walk and text at the same time. If you've ever bumped into a tree, person, car, or vicious squirrel while texting, this app is for you. Type n Walk lets you view your surroundings with your iPhone's built-in camera as you type. When you are done with your message, simply cut and paste it, and you can send it however you want: text, e-mail, or tweet.

*   *   *

The Color of Sweat

When hippopotami float around in water on hot days, it can look like they are sweating blood. They're not. The reddish-orangish liquid that hippos sweat out of their skin glands while in the sun is actually a self-made sunscreen that isn't blood-related at all. Hippo sweat is made of *hipposudoric* acid (red) and *norhipposudoric* acid (orange). Both of these things help fight against dehydration and bacterial infections.

Did you know? A mosquito's wings beat at about 300 to 600 times per second.

WORLD'S WEIRDEST MYTHS

Sure...you've heard of Bigfoot and the Loch Ness Monster. But compared to these mythical creatures? They're perfectly normal.

THE CREATURE: Vampire Cat

WHERE IT LIVES: Japan

THE MYTH: According to Japanese folklore, an ancient prince and his lady friend, Otoyo, were hanging out one evening when a cat began to follow them around. When Otoyo retired to bed, the cat attacked her throat and took on her human form. The demon cat then preyed on the prince every night, drinking his blood while he slept, until a common soldier hunted down Otoyo and killed her. A possible offshoot of this myth: the Japanese belief that if a person kills a cat, the cat's spirit will curse him unless he eats part of the dead animal before it can. (Ugh!)

THE CREATURE: Rat King

WHERE IT LIVES: Europe

THE MYTH: In the mid-1300s the Black Plague spread a fear of rats across Europe after it became clear that they were spreading the disease. Out of this fear arose the myth of the "rat king"—a creature made up of dozens to hundreds of wriggling rats, all somehow joined together at the tails. Could such a creature be real?

Museums in Germany and France show preserved specimens of rat kings that consist of seven to nine animals with interconnected tails—but science has yet to confirm the rat king as a real creature.

THE CREATURE: Death Worm

WHERE IT LIVES: Mongolia

THE MYTH: Legend has it the Death Worm lives beneath the burning sands of the Gobi Desert. The *olgoi-khorkhoi*— as it is known to Mongolians—looks like a cross between a venomous snake and an electric eel. Locals describe the creature as being three to five feet long and bright red, with electrically charged skin and dangerously acidic saliva. Dozens of Mongolians have reported sightings of the Death Worm, and several cryptozoologists (mythical beast hunters) have launched investigations. Results so far? No one has captured photographic proof of the beast.

THE CREATURE: *Konaki Jiji*

WHERE IT LIVES: Japan

THE MYTH: The name *konaki-jiji* translates to "old man crying like a baby." When the shape-shifting creature wants to lure victims, it transforms from an old man into a baby. Then it lies down by the side of the road and bawls its eyes and lungs out until some unsuspecting traveler picks it up to soothe it. That's when the creature swells to a 700-pound monster baby and crushes its well-meaning rescuer. An encounter with the konaki-jiji can have a silver lining, though. If the rescuer continues holding the baby after it blows up in size, that person will receive "magical gifts."

QUACKY GROWNUPS

Proof that you don't have to be boring to be an adult.

CRUNCH TIME

Some folks are addicted to chocolate. David Gracer from Providence, Rhode Island, has a thing for…insects. "I get told that I'm crazy, or sick, or weird," says the English teacher and father of two. According to Gracer, he's chowed down on 5,000 species so far. His favorites? Fly pupa, cockroaches, and scorpions. "Insects are loaded with vitamins," says Gracer. They're also "lower in fat than beef."

GOING PRUNEY

Know how your hands get all wrinkly after you're in the tub too long? At age 30, Tim Yarrow wasn't worried much about his hands when he dropped into a water-filled tank in a Johannesburg, South Africa, shopping mall in November 2002. He was hoping to set a new world record for being underwater, and he was worried about one thing: staying alive. To set a record, he'd have to breathe, eat, pee, and poop…all without leaving the water. Scuba gear took care of the breathing, a feeding tube provided nutrients, and a catheter—a tube stuck into places we won't mention—took care of elimination. But even though he wasn't worrying about going pruney, he did. By the end of his tank time, Yarrow's hands looked like giant snow-white wrinkled prunes. According to British ecologist Ellie Harrison, our hands and feet have extra layers of dead keratin cells on them. Those dead cells work like a sponge, absorbing water much faster than any other cells. "Because they're attached to the live keratin cells beneath, they just puff up and end up having to wrinkle. There's nowhere else for them to go." How long did it take Tim Yarrow's hands to turn into puffy prunes? Ten and a half days. (And, yes, he set a new world record. And, no, you should not try this at home.)

QUACK UP

Julie Ostrow likes to laugh…a lot. On April 6, 2013, the 46-year-old swimming instructor from Chicago faced off against a dozen hopefuls for the First American Laughing Championship. Ostrow went one-on-one against her opponents in four categories: the belly laugh, the Alabama knee slapper, the maniacal laugh, and the diabolical laugh. But after laughing her way into the finals, Ostrow had a big problem: "I couldn't stop laughing," she said. "I was afraid I'd die from laughing in front of the audience." Her face turned beet red, and tears spurted from her eyes as wave after wave of uncontrollable laughter shook her.

Ostrow's fear isn't ungrounded: there have been a number of recorded cases of death-by-laughter. In the third century B.C., a Greek philosopher named Chrysippus laughed himself to death after getting his donkey drunk and watching it try to eat figs. And in 1975, a bricklayer named Alex Mitchell laughed for nearly a half an hour, collapsed on the couch in front of his TV, and died. Mitchell's laughing fit was set off by a comedy skit involving a kilt-clad Scotsman fighting off a black pudding with nothing but his bagpipes. As for Julie Ostrow, luckily, she didn't die. Instead, she won the title of "Best Laugher in America."

NOT CHEAP

How comfortable is a bird's nest? An engineer, a naturalist, and an ornithologist (someone who studies birds) decided to find out. In 2011 they built a human-sized hummingbird nest in Chicago's Lincoln Park Zoo. "We built it with bungee cords and bean canes, and stuffed it with duvets, feathers, and pillows," says James Cooper, the engineer. Was it comfortable? Cooper doesn't really know. "Basically, it was three stupid Englishmen trying to behave like hummingbirds," he said. The nest was so small he ended up sleeping on the ground listening to lions roar nearby.

*   *   *

DUMB DOGNAPPER

In January 2013, 18-year-old Christopher Young walked up to a woman walking her Yorkshire Terrier on a street in Washington, D.C. "Give me your dog," Young demanded. "Yorkies cost a lot of money." Young was right: Yorkies go for as much as $1,500. But when he was counting his potential take, he didn't take into account his own clumsiness. As he snatched the dog, Young dropped his cell phone. While he scrambled to find it, the Yorkie slipped out of his grasp and ran for home. Young fled, but the dropped cell phone led police to information about another valuable device: the GPS-enabled ankle bracelet he was wearing for committing another crime. The bracelet not only pinpointed his exact location but—because it had been tracking his every step—gave law enforcement the evidence needed to lock Young up for armed robbery. With a four-year sentence, he might have just enough time to figure out the true cost of dumb.

Q: Who stole the soap?

LIGHT 'EM UP

Just so you know...Uncle John says, "It's not nice to make fun of people." Funny...but not nice.

Q: How many punk rockers does it take to change a lightbulb?
A: Two. One to change the bulb and one to smash the old bulb against his forehead.

Q: How many pro football players does it take to change a lightbulb?
A: One. But eleven get paid for doing it.

Q: How many Russians does it take to change a lightbulb?
A: Sorry. That is a carefully guarded state secret.

Q: How many surrealists does it take to change a lightbulb?
A: Mango.

Q: How many tech-support people does it take to change a lightbulb?
A: Did you try upgrading?

Lightbulb 1.3 will probably fix the problem.

Q: How many waiters does it take to change a lightbulb?
A: You're kidding, right? Even a burned-out lightbulb can't catch a waiter's eye.

Q: How many software engineers does it take to change a lightbulb?
A: None. It's a hardware problem.

Q: How many magicians does it take to change a lightbulb?
A: Depends on what you want to change it into.

Q: How many therapists does it take to change a lightbulb?
A: None. The lightbulb has to *want* to change.

A: The robber ducky!

WHAT "A" BABE

Warning: Being stubborn can sometimes backfire...even when you're on track to becoming a world-famous athlete.

"TYPE A"

Multi-sport sensation Mildred "Babe" Didrikson Zaharias may be the greatest woman athlete of all time, but the record-smashing day at a national track meet that earned her a trip to the 1932 Olympics almost didn't happen. There were no professional sports teams for women during the Depression era. Babe worked as a typist by day for the Dallas Employers Casualty insurance company. After work, she played semi-pro basketball for the company's team and competed in track and field events on weekends.

Babe was as speedy on the typewriter as she was in athletics. After she led the Employers Casualty team to a national basketball championship, she pressed her employer for a raise and an extra week's vacation. Her boss and coach—Colonel Melvorne McCombs—refused, so Babe quit and hopped a train home to Beaumont, Texas.

Didrikson's story might have ended there, but during the train ride, Babe realized she'd made a huge mistake. The upcoming Women's National Track and Field Championships doubled as the 1932 Olympic trials. Babe could not compete without the sponsorship of Employers Casualty. She took the next train back to Dallas and said "sorry" to Colonel McCombs.

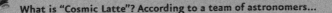

STANDING ALONE

Certain that Babe would win every event and become an Olympic standout, McCombs entered her in a record eight events as a "one-girl track team." But the night before the national meet near Chicago, Babe got so worked up she couldn't sleep or calm her fluttering stomach. "When I put a hand on it," Babe said, "the hand would just bounce up and down." The "team" chaperone called a doctor who diagnosed the trouble as a whopping case of nerves.

Because they didn't sleep well, Babe and the chaperone overslept. They rushed into a cab and sped to Dyche Stadium with Babe changing into her uniform behind a towel held up by the chaperone. Once they arrived, Babe dashed onto the field, waving to the audience when her company's name was announced. When the crowd realized Babe had no teammates, it went wild.

Her competitors, on the other hand, were not pleased. The temperature inside the stadium hovered around 100 degrees. The other athletes sat on a block of ice trying to keep cool—and when Babe arrived, they combusted. They complained to officials that the rules had been stretched to let her compete in eight events. The rules clearly stated that all athletes were limited to three.

ALL OVER THE FIELD

The competition had reason to worry about Didrikson. She rushed from event to event, smashing her own world records and winning five gold medals, including the 80-meter hurdles, the baseball throw, and the javelin. Babe also tied for first in the high jump. In fact, she missed medaling in only two of the eight events—the discus and the 100-meter sprint.

from Johns Hopkins University, it's the color of the universe.

Didrikson won the meet single-handedly, as Colonel McCombs predicted, earning more points than the second-place team's 22 competitors combined. "It was one of those days in an athlete's life when you know you're just right," Babe said. "You feel you could fly. You're like a feather floating in the air."

United Press International called it "The most amazing series of performances ever accomplished by any individual, male or female, in track and field history."

A BIGGER STAGE

Didrikson went on to win two gold medals (hurdles and javelin) and a silver (high jump) in the 1932 Olympic Games in Los Angeles. Soon after the Olympics, Babe was declared ineligible to compete as an amateur because Chrysler had used her name and picture in an advertisement for one of its cars.

As for her typist's job? She never did get a raise or an added week's vacation. It worked out for the best: Babe went on to become the most successful woman golfer in history, helping to found the Ladies Professional Golf Association (LPGA) and winning dozens of tournaments. She made more than a million dollars in her sports career, a huge amount in that era.

*   *   *

Q: Why did King Kong climb the Empire State Building?
A: He couldn't squeeze into the elevator.

Which came first? *Tyrannosaurus rex* is an ancestor of...the chicken!

LET THE BEDBUGS BITE

How far would you go for science? This guy went totally buggy!

BODY ART

Why did insect expert Johnny Fedora attach a bunny-rabbit stencil to the mouth of a jar containing 1,000 swarming bedbugs? We thought you'd never ask! The why: To create a temporary bedbug-bite tattoo. The how: Fedora simply turned the jar upside down and pressed it against his forearm, and 1,000 bugs made their way to the openings in the stencil to chow down on his arm. Fedora's an entomologist (bug scientist), so he knows his bugs. He says getting a bedbug tattoo is perfectly safe. Bedbugs don't transmit any diseases, and the red pus-filled blisters they leave behind when they feed on your arm heal in about two weeks. Itch-level on a scale of 1 to 10? At its worst, Fedora rates his itches at a 9. (Yikes!)

HOTEL SECURITY

Why did Fedora have a colony of bedbugs hanging out in a jar in his laboratory? The bugs were being used to train Bob, the bedbug-sniffing Beagle. Just as dogs can be trained to find bombs or bodies, they can also be trained to find bedbug infestations in hotel rooms. Fedora says it's all part of the "green revolution"—instead of spraying hotel rooms with potentially toxic chemicals to take care of bedbug problems, hoteliers can use bedbug-sniffing dogs like Bob to pinpoint problem beds for cleanup.

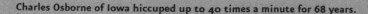

Charles Osborne of Iowa hiccuped up to 40 times a minute for 68 years.

TOYS GONE WRONG

Toys aren't what they used to be...which is probably a good thing.

TOY: Gilbert U-238 Atomic Energy Lab (1950s)
OOPS! In the early years of atomic energy, even scientists didn't fully understand its potential dangers. Maybe that explains why the University of Oakridge endorsed a kit that contained four types of uranium ore, its very own Geiger counter, and a comic book called *Learn How Dagwood Splits the Atom.* The kit was banned from toy stores in 1951 out of fear that some kids might eat the radioactive substances.

TOY: Sky Rangers Park Flyer (2005–2006)
OOPS! Made in China and sold in hobby stores for $20–$40, these light blue remote-controlled airplanes had a 14-inch wingspan. In 2007 the Consumer Product Safety Commission forced the plane's U.S. distributor to recall about 21,000 airplanes. According to the safety agency, "The airplanes are launched by hand and can explode near the consumer's head, posing a risk of temporary hearing loss and injuries to eyes, face, and hands."

TOY: Austin Magic Pistol (late 1940s)
OOPS! The Magic Pistol shot ping-pong balls from its barrel. The problem: to propel those balls, the gun had to be loaded up with calcium carbide, a chemical that becomes extremely explosive when mixed with water. Second problem: firing the gun required

adding…water. In a burst of explosive fire, the magic pistol shot out the balls at a speed almost as fast as a speeding bullet. They were out of stores by 1950, but a few can be found today on eBay. Beware: many states now classify the toy as a "firearm." Though they're highly collectible and expensive these days, there aren't many available for purchase. Why? Many of the magic pistols sold in the '40s ruptured or exploded when kids fired them.

TOY: Remington-Derringer Buckle Gun (1959)
OOPS! In 1959 the Mattel Toy Corporation thought it would be fun to conceal a cap gun in a belt buckle. To fire the gun, all a kid had to do was stick out his (or her) belly. That made the gun pop out of the buckle and fire. Pow! The design wasn't perfect—with the safety off, even slight stomach movements could cause the gun to fire, sometimes right into the belly of the kid wearing it. After several kids burned their legs, the toy was banned.

TOY: Fisher-Price Power Wheels Motorcycles (2000)
OOPS! They might have looked like shiny motorized toys, but these Power Wheels were real machines. The problem? The gas pedals on these battery-powered rides often got stuck in "go" mode. Kids ended up with cuts, sprains, and broken bones. One even drove himself into his house at full speed. (He survived.)

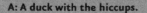

A: A duck with the hiccups.

In 2000 Fisher-Price took the "toy" off the market and recalled 218,000 of the danger-cycles.

TOY: Steve the Tramp (1990)
OOPS! Rev. Christopher Rose, rector of Grace Episcopal Church in Hartford, Connecticut, called the Steve the Tramp figure "one of the most offensive toys of the 1990 Christmas season." Who was Steve the Tramp? The character got his start in the long-running Dick Tracy comic strip set in the 1930s. Steve was a villain: a one-eyed vagrant, a drifter, and a sometimes kidnapper who sported a tattered checkered coat and a worn cloth cap. In the strip's later years, Steve redeemed himself by working in a soup kitchen feeding the homeless and helping out when some of them went missing.

In 1990 Disney's Touchstone Pictures turned *Dick Tracy* into a movie. Fourteen "coppers and gangsters" from the movie became five-inch-tall plastic figurines. The package copy for Steve the Tramp calls the character "an ignorant bum" and claims, "You'll smell him before you see him." That did not sit well with homeless advocates, including Marvin Minkler of Gateway Homeless Outreach, who helped organize a protest against the doll. Carlton Whitehorn, a soup kitchen volunteer involved in the protest, had a message for Disney: "I'm homeless, and you don't smell me before you see me. I'd like to let Disney know that Jesus Christ was homeless, too." The protest worked. Disney stopped producing the doll and, according to Minkler, promised to meet with Gateway to see how the company might collaborate on a program to help the homeless.

*   *   *

"My parents didn't want to move to Florida, but they turned sixty, and it was the law."—**Jerry Seinfield**

In Thailand, it is considered rude to use a fork while eating.

QUOTABLE KIDS

Before they were celebrities, they were just...kids.

"I was a pretty nerdy kid. I'm still kind of nerdy. I have all of the worst qualities of being a nerd—all of the affect and none of the smarts."

—**Claire Danes**

"I really had a lot of dreams when I was a kid, and I think a great deal of that grew out of the fact that I had a chance to read a lot."

—**Bill Gates**

"I think who you are in school really sticks with you. I don't ever feel like the cool kid at the party, ever. It's like, 'Smile and be nice to everybody because you were not invited to be here.'"

—**Taylor Swift**

"When I was a kid, whenever we skated my dad would not let us on the ice without hockey sticks because of this insane fear we would become figure skaters!"

—**Norm MacDonald**

"I really like grammar. And spelling. I was a spelling-bee kid. I'm hard-core about grammar."

—**Emma Stone**

"When I was a kid, my mother used to feed me mashed-potato sandwiches, brussels sprout sandwiches.... My brain cells were starving from lack of food. I'll eat anything. I'll eat dirt."

—**Sylvester Stallone**

BWA-A-AWK!

On page 212, we told you about some talented birds. Here are two more.

BIRD: Parrot
GIFT: Roman Emperor Basiliscus Macedo's pet parrot once embarrassed him during a banquet around the year A.D. 840. The Emperor had recently jailed his son, Leo, whom he thought was a traitor. Legend has it that—throughout the dinner party—the emperor's parrot continuously cried out, "Alas, alas! Poor Prince Leo!" The parrot's accusations made the banquet guests so uncomfortable they couldn't enjoy the feast. "How should we eat, Sire," one guest was reported to have said, "when we are thus reproached by this bird of our want of duty to your family? We have neglected to supplicate Your Majesty in behalf of the prince, whom we all believe to be innocent." Basiliscus Macedo's solution: He set his son free.

BIRD: Parrot
GIFT: What locals on London's Half Moon Street remembered most about Piccadilly the parrot was the bird's ability to sing with perfect pitch. "God Save the King" was one of her favorite tunes. If Piccadilly missed a note, she would go back and correct the part of the song she'd messed up and then sing to the end. Her owner, Irishman Colonel O'Kelly, refused many pricey offers to turn Piccadilly into a star. She died in 1802 at the ripe old parrot age of...well, no one knows exactly. What is known? O'Kelly owned her for more than 30 years, so Piccadilly had a lot of years to perfect her pitch. Doctors who dissected the bird after her death discovered abnormally strong throat muscles, probably created from her frequent singing.

SCHOOL'S OUT!

There can never be too many reasons for a day off from school.

- The good news: on March 3 Japan celebrates *Hina Matsuri* (Girls' Day or the Doll Festival). Families with daughters display special dolls clothed in the fancy dress of Japanese royalty. Girls put on their best kimonos and visit other families to admire their doll displays. The bad news? Girls' Day doesn't come with a day off school. Boys' Day—celebrated on May 5—does. On *Tangu No Sekku* (Children's Day or Boys' Day) Japanese families string huge streamers shaped like carp (a kind of fish) on long poles outside their homes—one carp for each male of the house. Some say *Tangu No Sekku* is boys' sweet revenge for putting up with Doll Day.

- Why do school kids in Bolivia get a day away from school on March 23? For Day of the Sea, a reminder to everyone that the country once had ocean access. Huh? Bolivia didn't move— the country lost its last link to the ocean in a battle against neighboring Chile that took place in 1904. Bolivians remember the painful defeat once a year, walking the streets and listening to the sound of sea gulls and ship's horns blasted from loud speakers.

- If kids want to wear shorts to school in Bermuda, they have to wait until May 24—Bermuda Day. Schools close on that day to allow Bermudians to enjoy parades, road races, and regattas. It's also the official day for donning Bermuda shorts. After Bermuda Day, kids can wear shorts for the rest of the school year instead of regulation trousers.

FUTURAMA

In 1899, Lord Kelvin (a British scientist) said, "Radio has no future. Heavier-than-air flying machines are impossible. X-rays will prove to be a hoax." As predictions go, that one's an epic fail and...so are these.

PREDICTION: "I think there is a world market for maybe five computers."—**IBM's Thomas Watson, 1943**
EPIC FAIL: Gartner, Inc., a technology research company, estimates that in 2013 there were 2.4 *billion* computer devices in use—that includes PCs, tablets, and smartphones. Watson only missed by 999,999,995 computers.

PREDICTION: "Space travel is bunk."—**Royal Astronomer Sir Harold Spencer Jones, 1957**
EPIC FAIL: Two weeks after Sir Harold's prediction, the Soviet Union successfully launched *Sputnik*, the world's first satellite, into space. Since that time, 12 people have walked on the surface of the moon. Crafts from Earth have landed on Venus, Mars, Jupiter, and on moons of Saturn and Mars. As of 2014, *Voyager I*, launched in 1977, had left Earth's solar system and headed into interstellar space, having reached a distance of 18 billion kilometers from our sun.

PREDICTION: "The world will end on May 11, 1992."—**Reverend Harold Camping, founder of Family Radio**
EPIC FAIL: Most of the readers of this book were born long after 1992, so we're guessing Camping got it wrong. That didn't stop him from trying again...and again...and again. Basing his calculations on numbers and dates found in the Bible,

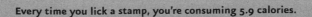

Camping next predicted that the world would end in mid-September of 1994. "I am ninety-nine point nine percent certain that my math is correct," Camping boasted. It wasn't. Camping's next prediction: Christ would return and the world would end on March 31, 1995. Uhmm...nope. So how about October 21, 2011? When the world failed to end on that day, Camping announced his retirement from predicting the end of the world. "I'm like the boy who cried wolf again and again, and the wolf didn't come," Camping told the *San Francisco Chronicle* in 1995. "It seems embarrassing." (You think?)

PREDICTION: A particle accelerator called the Hadron Collider might create a mini black hole that would swallow Earth.—**German chemist Otto Rössler, 2008**

EPIC FAIL: Around 14 billion years ago, our universe burst into being. Trying to learn more about Earth's beginning, CERN (the European Council for Nuclear Energy) designed and built the Hadron Collider. Once the collider went online, scientists could fire atomic particles around the collider's 17-mile long underground ring hoping to recreate the chemical reactions that took place when the universe formed. The particles would race around the collider at super speeds: so fast they'd make 11,245 trips around the ring every second, and then...they would collide head on. According to Rössler...potential cosmic *kaboom*!

If a mini black hole did form but did not instantly consume our planet, it could still cause "local change in the ionization of the atmosphere due to a microquasar-like micro-jet pointing out of the earth." If you're thinking, "Huh?" you're not alone. Let's just say, that would not be good news. Microquasars are the energy-spewing end of a black hole that pumps out deadly X-rays and radio waves. What did Rössler have to say about that? "Securing the survival of even a handful of human beings in case of a human-made Armageddon is a planet-wide duty. When the first unmistakable signs occur it is too late." His solution? Watch what the Chinese were up to. Rössler thought their plan to colonize the moon meant they agreed with him on the dangers of the Hadron Collider.

On September 1, 2008, Britain's *Sun* newspaper ran the headline "End of World Due in 9 Days." The particle accelerator was fired up on September 10th. Six years later, we're still waiting for those mini black holes or microquasars to materialize.

PREDICTION: "Within the next few decades, autos will have folding wings that can be spread when on a straight stretch of road so that the machine can take to the air."
—American WWI flying ace Eddie Rickenbacker, 1924
EPIC FAIL: Rickenbacker made his "flying car" prediction in an interview with *Popular Science* magazine in July 1924. Scientists, aviators, and inventors—including Henry Ford—have all tried and failed to put a flying car into American garages. A company called Terrfugia has gotten closest so far: It has developed a compact personal plane with foldable wings that can be flown into an airport and then driven home. It's far from the popular science fiction version of the flying car. "This isn't *The Jetsons*," said Terrafugia's Richard Gersh. "You cannot take off from your driveway."

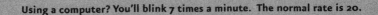

THINK BEFORE YOU INK!

A tip from Uncle John: Tattoos are permanent. So hire a tattoo artist who finished high school or skip the ink.

Prome Queen

I'M A MARSHIAN

Never don't give up

SEE YOU AT THE COSSROADS

**NOLEGE
IS
POWER**

What didn't killed me made me stronger!

**SUPER
XXXVIII
BOWEL**

MY MOM IS MY ANGLE

God grant me the serenity to accecpt the things I cannot change.

GO WHEREEVER THE WIND TAKES YOU

Live You're Life

TOO COOL FOR SCOOL

"You can lead a horse to water, but you can't make him float."—**Unknown**

Rabbits sweat through the pads in their feet.

INVENTIVE KIDS

*Some of the world's most useful inventions
come from the minds of kids.*

PATENTLY DANGEROUS

In 1849 New Englander Margaret "Mattie" Knight was working in a cotton mill when a shuttle flew off a loom, stabbed a boy, and killed him. Mattie was twelve at the time, and the accident shook her so badly she decided to make sure such a thing would never happen again. The details have been lost over time, but here's what is known: Mattie created a safety device that made it impossible for the shuttle to leave the loom. Pretty soon every new power shuttle came with Mattie's safety device. Did she get rich? No. Mattie didn't know that inventions could be patented, so she never earned a dime for her invention. The U.S. goverment grants patents to inventors "to exclude others from making, using, offering for sale, or selling the invention throughout the United States or importing the invention into the United States." An inventor has to apply for a patent and disclose how the invention works before a patent will be granted. After that, the inventor's right to make money from an invention is protected.

S'NO FUN

In Maine—where temperatures can drop to -50°F (-45.3°C)—kids learn how to build snow forts at an early age. Building snow forts leads to a discovery: winter fun includes wet soggy mittens and snow dripping down your sleeves. In 1994 after a day of snow fort building, ten-year-old KK Gregory decided she'd had enough.

She created Wristies: fingerless gloves made of cozy fleece that extend halfway up the arm to keep wrists warm and dry. Gregory asked her Girl Scout troop to test them out. The verdict? Wristies worked! Gregory's mom helped her get a patent for her invention, trademark the name "Wristies" so no one else could use it, and create a company to produce the wrist warmers.

ODOR EATER

Param Jaggi is always thinking. In 2008 he was thinking about the stinky exhaust fumes belching out of the car sitting in front of him at a stop sign in Plano, Texas. That's when he got the idea for his first invention: a CO_2-eating algae machine. Jaggi was fifteen at the time. He calls his invention "Algae Mobile." How does it work? Algae Mobile plugs into a car's tailpipe. Carbon dioxide-filled exhaust passes through plates of algae inside the device. The algae turn it into oxygen before releasing it into the air. The cost: $30. Right now, Algae Mobile is still in the testing stage. But the young inventor has already applied for a patent to protect his rights.

CRAYON RESCUE

In 1991 eleven-year-old Cassidy Goldstein was working on a crayon-drawn masterpiece. But she had a problem: all the crayons in her art box were broken. Instead of throwing the crayons away and asking her parents to buy new ones, Cassidy came up with an idea—crayon holders. She'd noticed the plastic water tubes her mom used to keep flowers fresh and decided they might work for holding stubby crayons. When they did, Cassidy grilled several patent lawyers about her idea, applied for a patent, and then licensed her idea to a company that could manufacture the holders.

Cassidy's invention put her through college and inspired her dad to start a company to help other kid inventors.

THIS LITTLE PIGGY WENT TO THE STOCK MARKET

Fabian Fernandez-Han won the New York Stock Exchange Financial Future Challenge for inventing "Oink-a-Saurus," an app that teaches kids about managing money. Here's how it works: Oink-a-Saurus tracks what a user looks at online or buys from online stores. The app gathers information about the user's interests and spending habits. Then it calculates how much a user might have earned by saving or investing the money instead of spending it. "Kids spend huge amounts of money on things they don't need when they should be saving and investing for their future, such as college," Fabian says. On January 11, 2010, Fabian got to ring the closing bell at the NYSE stock exchange for winning the challenge. He also pocketed a $2,500 prize, which we're guessing went straight into his own piggy bank (or investment portfolio).

*   *   *

HIC-C-C-C-UP!

They start when the vagus nerve running from your brain to your belly gets irritated. Here's how to stop them:

1. Eat a spoonful of sugar or vinegar.

2. Put your fingers in your ears.

3. Take a small sip of hot sauce.

4. Stick out your tongue as far as you can.

5. Sing as loudly as you can.

6. Hold your nose and mouth closed as if you were about to jump into a pool.

7. Blow on your thumb as if you were blowing into a balloon.

DOOMED TO FAIL

Some TV shows were always destined for the video graveyard.

SHOW: *Little Muppet Monsters*

If Muppets are good, double the Muppets must be better...at least that's what CBS execs thought when they expanded the *Muppet Babies* series from a half-hour show to an hour-long block. They paired *Muppet Babies* with a new show, *Little Muppet Monsters*, to make an hour-long package called *Muppets, Babies and Monsters.*

WHY IT DIDN'T WORK: Muppets, Muppets, and more Muppets. Seems the combination of all kinds of Muppets—babies, adults, and monsters—plus live puppet Muppets *and* animated cartoon Muppets was...let's just say...very confusing to viewers. Also, production was rushed and it didn't meet Muppet creator Jim Henson's high standards. Though they had 18 episodes ready to go, Henson mercifully pulled the block from the Saturday morning lineup after the third episode.

SHOW: *Garbage Pail Kids*

In 1985 Topps Garbage Pail Kids were the world's hottest non-sports trading cards. The cards made fun of the cute dough-faced Cabbage Patch Kid dolls that were popular at the time. Each trading card featured a disgusting Garbage Pail Kid character with an equally horrifying name, such as Adam Bomb, Scotty Potty, or Clogged Duane.

WHY IT DIDN'T WORK: Critics said the show was gross, ridiculed the handicapped, and glorified violence. It got bumped from the CBS schedule following protests from a number of groups,

including Action for Children's Television, the National Coalition on Television Violence, and the Christian Leaders for Responsible Television. Sponsors such as Nabisco, McDonalds, and Crayola pulled out under pressure from these and other groups. However, the show did air in several other countries, including Spain, Brazil, England, Iceland, and Israel. Reportedly, with few complaints.

SHOW: *Allen Gregory*

The Fox Network became king of the TV cartoons with edgy young characters like Stewie Griffin (*Family Guy*) and Bart Simpson (*The Simpsons*). But they went wrong with an unlikable seven-year-old named Allen Gregory De Longpre. *Allen Gregory* premiered

in 2011, and the main character was the cartoon alter ego of Jonah Hill, one of the show's creators.

WHY IT DIDN'T WORK: Unlike Stewie and Bart, Allen wasn't funny. Or was he? Viewers weren't really sure if the writers were trying to make the show's star funny...or not. What was he? According to one reviewer, he was "jerky, snide, socially inept, and perversely twisted." *Allen Gregory* received mostly negative reviews from critics, including this one from *USA Today*'s Robert Bianco: "Gross, ugly, vicious, and stupid—Allen is all of that, to be sure. But funny? Too rarely to matter." The show was dumped after seven episodes. As for creator Jonah Hill, he didn't seem thrown by losing his alter ego. "Our central love story is between a six-year-old kid and a hideous 80-year-old lady, you know? I feel really prideful that we got that on the air."

Hey, Fish Lips! Most lipstick contains fish scales.

SHOW: *Battletoads*

Battletoads was the story of three nerdy junior high school students from Oxnard, California, unfortunately named after skin conditions: Rash, Zitz, and Pimple. They were turned into *anthropomorphic* (talking animal) toads with superhuman strength. Bizarrely, they could change their arms and legs into weapons such as buzzing sawblades and crashing cymbals. Their crime-fighting assignment? Save a princess named Angelica from the evil Dark Queen.

WHY IT DIDN'T WORK: Can you say "rip-off"? If *Battletoads* wasn't a blatant attempt to capitalize on the popularity of TV's most famous band of mutant amphibians—the Teenage Mutant Ninja Turtles—Uncle John will eat a toad. The *Battletoads* video game was a success. The TV show...a flop. The pilot that aired didn't get picked up by a network. It did, however, win an "honor" of sorts: In 2008 *Battletoads* took fifth place on Topless Robot's list of "5 Worst One-Shot TV Cartoons Ever Made."

*　　*　　*

A BIG STINK

Everybody farts, right? But not everyone gets into trouble for serial farting at work. That's what happened to one poor guy at the Social Security Administration in Washington, D.C. After his manager logged in 60 stink bombs over 17 days (by date and time), he put the guy on notice for causing "a hostile work environment." The worker received an official reprimand accusing him of disrupting the workplace by "passing gas and releasing an unpleasant odor." According to the reprimand, such behavior is "Conduct Unbecoming a Federal Employee."

Comedian Jack Black's parents were both...rocket scientists.

WORLD'S QUACKIEST WEDDINGS

When you attend a wedding, you expect the bride to come down the aisle dressed in a white bridal gown. It's tradition, after all. These days, some brides have more...creative ideas.

YUM, YUM!

Why not skip the dress and go straight for the dessert? That might be what pastry chef Valentyn Shtefano was thinking when he designed a wedding dress for his fiancée in 2006. Shtefano made the floor-length gown out of cream puffs baked with flour, eggs, sugar, and caramel. The creation took two months of work and 1,500 cream puffs. The bride, Viktoriya, modeled the gown for several hours every night as Shtefano added more and more cream puffs to fill in the shape.

Another chef, Juan Manuel Barrientos from Colombia, made two edible wedding gowns. Instead of using cream puffs, Barrientos formed his dresses with sugar-glazed flowers and rose petals. By the time he was done, each dress had more than 2,000 sugar petals. To prove they were completely edible, Barrientos took small bites from his creations when he displayed them at design shows.

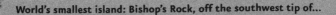

FLUSH OF HAPPINESS

If making wedding dresses from food seems weird, how about toilet paper? Every year, the Charmin toilet paper company sponsors a contest to see who can create the best wedding dress out of glue, tape, thread, and good old TP. The winner gets a cushy $2,000, and more than 700 contestants compete each year. Artist Susan Brennan has won the contest twice. One of her creations took 10 jumbo rolls of TP and 100 hours of work. The gown ended up looking like a layer cake covered in fluffy sugary ruffles. "The bottom looks like frosting—delicious!" Brennan says. She didn't stop when the dress was finished, either—she used more squeezeably soft paper to make a matching purse, headband, bracelet, and brooch.

HAIR COMES THE BRIDE

Say what you will about toilet-paper wedding dresses, at least you end up with something that looks like a traditional gown. Most non-traditional dressmaking material we found? Human hair. In 2011 designer Thelma Madine teamed up with a stylist and a beauty salon to make a wedding gown entirely out of hair extensions. She chose the wildest colors—fire-engine red, deep mahogany, neon pink, and golden blonde. None of those colors say "white wedding." Madine thinks it would be the perfect gown for singer-entertainer Lady Gaga. "I'd be overwhelmed if Lady Gaga would consider wearing it," Madine told the *Daily Mail Reporter*. The "hair dress," as it came to be called, took eight people 300 hours and three months to build. It's made of 250 meters of hair, which weigh more than 30 pounds. Its 12 layers of puffy hair skirts make the dress just as wide as it is tall.

QUACKED NEWS

And you thought reading the news was boring!

• When police in Aachen, Germany, spotted a VW Beetle parked in a "no parking" zone, they tried brushing off the license plate to read the number so they could ticket the vehicle. The problem? It wasn't a real car. It was a VW Beetle sculpted entirely out of snow.

• Fifty-nine-year-old Yolanda Arguello made very special cheese sandwiches for the probation and parole officers at the South Valley New Mexico Women's Recovery Academy. How special? First, she licked the cheese slices. Then she put the slices on the sandwiches and served them to the officers. She's been charged with three counts of battery on a peace officer.

• Scott Brierley, 23, was touring West Midlands Safari Park in England when he tried to take a photo of a 22-year-old elephant and dropped his cell phone. Keepers ordered him to stay in his car and keep moving. The last thing he saw? The elephant walking toward his phone. Brierley must have thought the huge animal would crush the phone, but it didn't. Instead, it picked up the phone in its trunk and... took a selfie. Brierley found the photo when park keepers returned his cell phone.

• Passengers aboard a US Airways flight from Los Angeles to Philadelphia in May, 2014, cringed when a service dog pooped right in the cabin aisle. Crew members tried to clean up the mess, but they couldn't do much about the smell. An hour later, it happened again. This time the stench was so bad passengers started dry-heaving. "A couple of people were throwing up," passenger Steve McCall told *Inside Edition*. When the crew ran out of paper towels, the pilot made an emergency landing for doggy-doo cleanup.

• In May 2014, McDonald's rolled out a new Happy Meal mascot. It looked like a red box with a gaping mouthful of teeth and golden-arches eyebrows sprouting above big googly eyes. The idea: bring "fun and excitement to children's meals." The problem: it didn't. Instead, the mascot's cavernous mouth and rows of big teeth brought shivers. "It's the meal that eats you," said one Happy Meal buyer.

• Bowls of nuts set out for Queen Elizabeth II at Buckingham palace seemed to empty out much faster than Her Royal Highness could eat them. The Queen suspected palace police of munching her treats and decided to catch them. How? She marked the sides of the bowls so she could see if the levels dipped. They did. The furious Queen sent word that officers should "keep their sticky fingers out."

• In 2013 life imitated the Tom Hanks movie *The Terminal*. A Syrian man named Wasfi Tayseer Jarad got stuck in Terminal 2 of the Dubai airport. Jarad had been serving a prison term. By the time he got out, his passport had expired. He bathed in airport restrooms and lived on a hamburger a day while waiting for a new passport. How long did he wait? Sixteen days.

...Mongol warrior Genghis Khan. He has 16 million descendants alive today.

ASK THE EXPERTS

Have a weird question? There's always an expert with an answer.

UG-G-G-GH!

Q: *Why does breath smell bad in the morning?*

A: "Even if you are not prone to bad breath (*halitosis* is the medical term for stench mouth), yours will still smell kind of funky when you wake up in the morning. Morning breath is the result of a dry mouth. When you sleep, your salivary glands reduce their production of saliva. Why does a dry mouth smell? One answer is that your spit helps cleanse the mouth. It contains antibiotics and antimicrobials that kill many of the nasty, stinky germs that live there. During the night, these little guys can flourish. You also swallow less when you sleep. Swallowing takes away a lot of these bacteria and their wastes." (*Disgusting Things: A Miscellany* by Don Voorhees)

AR-R-R-RGH!

Q: *Why does the screech of a chalkboard send chills up my spine?*

A: "In 1986, three U.S. researchers conducted four experiments to test the *psychoacoustics* (the study of how sounds affect people) of 'blackboard screech.' The original theory that blackboard screech produces chills simply because of its high frequency quickly fell by the wayside. When researchers removed the high frequencies, it had no effect on the unpleasant reactions experienced. In fact, when the lower frequencies were removed, the sound that was left was judged by subjects in the experiment to be rather pleasing. Next, the researchers experimented with the volume,

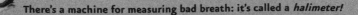

There's a machine for measuring bad breath: it's called a *halimeter!*

but the volume had no bearing on the chilling effect. Finally, they compared the blackboard screech with a variety of sounds found in nature and discovered that blackboard screech bears a remarkable resemblance to the warning cries emitted by a species of lower-order primates: Japanese macaques. This result suggested to the researchers that our tingling spines may be a primitive reflex left over from an earlier phase of our evolutionary history. It is also possible that blackboard screech may be similar to the sound made by some sort of prehistoric predator." (*The Odd Body: Mysteries of Our Weird and Wonderful Bodies Explained* by Stephan Juan)

PH-H-H-H-T!

Q: *What animal lets the biggest farts?*

A: "In 2003, Nick Gales, lead research scientist in the Applied Maritime Mammal Ecology Group of the Australian Antarctic Division, was on an expedition between Marguerite Bay and Palmer Station, collecting whale turds in order to find out what the whales were eating. Standing on the bow of the NB *Palmer*, Gales was practically on top of a whale when it let loose with a wet one. As Gales later told Benson, 'We got away from the bow of the ship very quickly…it does stink.'" (*Blame it on the Dog: A Modern History of the Fart* by Jim Dawson)

*　　*　　*

"The most remarkable thing about my mother is that for thirty years she served the family nothing but leftovers. The original meal has never been found."—**Calvin Trillin, American humorist**

What kills 4 times as many people a year as sharks? Vending machines!

ANIMAL ANTICS

And you thought humans had all the fun....

STAGE FRIGHT

If you had an Amazon parrot that could sing pop songs and had a vocabulary of 50 words and phrases, would you pass up the chance to try out for *America's Got Talent?* Bird trainer Sarah Hoeft certainly didn't. When she got the call to enter the 2011 season with her parrot, Echo, Hoeft went for it. She figured that five years performing at Wisconsin's Animal Gardens had prepared the parrot for the big time. At first, it seemed Hoeft was right: Echo sang his way straight into the semifinals. But the pressure of having a larger-than-usual audience, plus the fact that his girlfriend, Binky, was watching, caused Echo to freeze up in the middle of singing "Somewhere over the Rainbow." Hoeft took the loss in stride.

TOTALLY SQUIRRELLY

When it comes to Sugar Bush the squirrel, former champion baton twirler Kelly Foxton of Boca Raton, Florida, controls the antics. Foxton spends 12 hours a day collecting squirrel-sized costumes, props, and stage sets for Sugar Bush. Over the past 12 years, she has collected around 4,000 outfits, complete with wigs, hats, and shoes. Among the squirrel's getups: a Red Cross nurse, the Statue of Liberty, the Phantom of the Opera, and a toilet-repairing plumber. Dressed in the outfit-of-the-day, Sugar Bush poses for so many photos he's become "the world's most photographed" bushy-tailed rodent. Why does Foxton do it? "You've got to have a reason to get up in the morning and a reason to go to bed late at night," she says.

On average, your heart beats 100,000 times per day.

DOGTV

Workdays can be tough for a dog. While its humans are away, Fido is stuck at home. What's a dog to do? Watch television! Not just any channel, but DOGTV. Years of consulting with the world's top pet experts helped DOGTV's founder, Ron Levi, create content designed for a dog's special vision and hearing. DOGTV features 3- to 6-minute clips with mood-enhancing music, all designed to relax, stimulate, or comfort dogs with scenes from everyday life. What kind of clips? Dogs racing on a beach, dogs retrieving balls, dogs balancing on the tips of surfboards, dogs getting their necks rubbed...and lots of clips of dogs playing with dogs. "Dogs enjoy seeing other dogs on TV," says Levi. "And they love classical music. It helps put them to sleep."

OH...RATS!

There's nothing unusual about circus animals. But circus rats? In 1979 a former lion and tiger tamer named Henri Gugelmann introduced "the world's first rat circus" in Bern, Switzerland. These rats didn't just crawl around and squeak. While Gugelmann directed in a clown suit, his eleven-member troop of trained rats jumped over ropes, leaped through burning rings, and raced around a rat-sized track. The rat circus's big top is mobile: Gugelmann pedals it around town on a flat-topped bicycle-drawn cart. Why did Gugelmann switch from lions and tigers to rats? He was mauled by one of his former performers and decided to switch to a safer act.

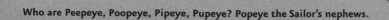

POOP-U-LAR SCIENCE

Though the lowly pile of poop doesn't look like much, it may provide a medical miracle—and even create renewable energy.

A POOP-U-LAR COLOR

Diagnosing stomach problems could soon be as easy (and disgusting) as looking in the toilet bowl. The key: a new variety of bacteria known as *E chromi*. Scientists experimenting in synthetic biology produced the bacteria in a lab. When these bacteria pass through your digestive tract, they react with the enzymes, proteins, and other chemicals that are present. That causes them to turn different colors, and those colors make diagnosing illness as simple as matching colors to a chart.

It's easy to get *E chromi* into your digestive system. Just guzzle down a yogurt-like shake filled with the engineered bacteria. Once the bacteria reacts with the chemicals in your gut, your next visit to the bathroom could let you know whether you've got a tummy ache or something far more serious. Blue poop means you might have worms (yuk!). Purple poop? Salmonella. Green? Colorectal cancer. As for "classic brown"…all is well, so flush it down!

POOP TRANSPLANT

In the U.S., more than 14,000 die every year from *Clostridium difficile.* What's that? It's a kind of bacterium that causes uncontrollable super diarrhea. These rod-shaped bacteria live in the world around us—even in our guts. Because the "good bacteria" living in our bodies keep *C. difficile* in check, they usually cause no problems. Add antibiotics to the mix and the results can be disastrous...even deadly. Antibiotics kill or stop the growth of disease-causing microorganisms. They also kill off the "good bacteria" in our guts. When that happens, *C. difficile* populations grow unchecked. The result: Toxins produced by the bacteria can cause serious illness and even death.

The good news: Researchers have found a solution. The bad news: The solution involves a poop transplant. (We're not kidding.) First, doctors collect crap from one of a patient's close relatives. Next, they mix the collected poo with saline—a sterile saltwater solution—or milk. Then (hang onto your barf bags) they place the poop into the patient's digestive system. How? Through a tube inserted up the patient's anus (butt) or down through the patient's mouth. Early tests of the procedure (appropriately named RePOOPulate) show regrowth of "good bacteria" in patients' guts within three days.

POO POWER

Here's a fact: Americans flush 15 trillion gallons of sewage down the toilet…every day. More than half of that is processed into sludge that fertilizes farmland, lawns, and home vegetable gardens. But sewage can also be a great source of *biogas*, a renewable energy source that can help generate electricity. That's why an increasing number of cities have begun to explore "poop-to-power" plants to generate energy.

According to one estimate, a single American's daily sludge output can generate enough electricity to light a 60-watt bulb for

Lock up! About half of all regular cyclists have their bikes stolen.

more than nine hours. Sound strange? Surprisingly, making power from human waste is nothing new. Experts say biogas was used to heat bath water in Assyria in the tenth century B.C. and in Persia in the sixteenth century. In the thirteenth century, Marco Polo noted that the Chinese used covered sewage tanks to generate power, while biogas technologies were also mentioned by seventeenth century author Daniel Defoe.

From flush to finish, the biogas process takes about 23 days. As for the smell, don't worry. Biogas smells just like the standard natural gas supply—in other words…like rotten eggs.

* * *

MORE TV TALK

On page 79 we shared quotes about the device that sometimes interrupts your bathroom reading. If those didn't send you back to books, here are a few more.

"I find television very educational. The minute somebody turns it on, I go into the library and read a good book."

—**Groucho Marx**

"Stop with the reality television. If I wanted reality, I'd take the screen out of my TV and look through the box.""

—**Jerry Seinfeld**

"Television is a triumph of equipment over people, and the minds that control it are so small that you could put

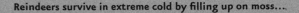

Reindeers survive in extreme cold by filling up on moss….

them in a gnat's navel with room left over for two caraway seeds and an agent's heart."
—**Fred Allen**

"On Friday night, I was reading my new book, but my brain got tired, so I decided to watch some television instead."
—**Stephen Chbosky**

"The technique is wonderful. I didn't even dream it would be so good. I would never let my children come close to the thing."
—**Vladimir Zworkin, the "Father of Television"**

"If everyone demanded peace instead of another television set, then there'd be peace."
—**John Lennon**

"Have you noticed that TV families never watch television?"
—**Henny Youngman**

"If the television craze continues with the present level of programs, we are destined to have a nation of morons."
—**Daniel Marsh, President of Boston University, 1950**

"Everything is for the eye these days—TV, *Life*, *Look*, the movies. Nothing is just for the mind. The next generation will have eyeballs as big as cantaloupes and no brain at all."—**Fred Allen**

"So, please, oh please, we beg, we pray, go throw your TV set away, and in its place you can install a lovely bookcase on the wall."
—**Roald Dahl**

*   *   *

Q: What do ducks watch on TV?
A: Duckumentaries!

FURBY FEVER

In 1998 a toy that looked like a fuzzy alien owl with bunny ears turned Christmas season into a feeding frenzy. Here's the story!

ROBOT DREAMS

In 1996 inventor David Hampton watched the Tamogotchi craze sweep through Japan. The egg-shaped handheld digital "pets" required nearly constant care. If a kid didn't feed his or her virtual pet, it could starve to death within half an hour. (What fun!) Hampton decided to take digital buddies to the next level: He would invent a robotic friend that would "respond, learn, sing, play games, and move while displaying rudimentary artificial intelligence." Hampton teamed up with fellow toy inventor Richard C. Levy to design the robot friend of his dreams.

The designers came up with a furry white owl-like creature that could wiggle its ears and open and close its huge eyes. Furby came out of the box speaking its own language: Furbish. "U-nye-boh-doo?" translated to "How are you?" "Wee-tee-kah-wah-tee" meant "Sing me a song." Most amazing to kids and parents? Furby could "listen to" and gradually "learn" English! Except…not really. The robot pet was programmed to use more English words over time to make kids *think* it was learning the language.

FURBY FUR FLIES

Less than two years later—in 1998—Furby went on sale at FAO Schwarz in New York City. Within a week, not only had the toy store sold every Furby in stock, it had back orders for 35,000 more Furbies. By the end of the holiday season, buyers had scooped

Hate veggies? Then eat pumpkins, cucumbers, eggplant…

up 1.8 million Furbys. What's bad about that? Scores of wannabe Furby buyers were left standing in line, empty-handed.

Because of the high demand, stores ran out of Furbies as soon as shipments arrived. Police had to be called in to separate two "Furby fighters" in New Smyrna Beach, Florida. In an O'Fallon, Illinois, Wal-Mart, a pre-Christmas stampede led to the injury of two women. In Denver, Colorado, frantic Furby shoppers knocked over displays and trampled bystanders.

"If kindergarten kids acted like that, they'd have to have a time-out," said Dr. Gregory Fritz, director of child and adolescent psychiatry at Brown University.

BUYERS BEWARE

Disappointed customers turned to auction sites like eBay to score a Furby. Prices soared from the suggested $35 retail price to hundreds of dollars. But inflated prices weren't the worst thing consumers ran into trying to buy Furbies. What was? Scammers. According to Jim Lanford, co-editor of *Internet ScamBusters*, consumers lost more than $5 million buying fake Furbies or ordering Furbies that were never delivered. "The real number is probably two to four times that amount," said Lanford. One scammer alone—Pennsylvanian David Saunders—took orders from as many as 400 people, never intending to deliver Furbies to any of them.

Other scammers listed "rare" or "collectible" Furbies for sale. At the time, Lana Simon, spokesperson for Tiger Electronics (the toy's maker) sent out this warning to buyers: "There are no rare Furbies and no collectible Furbies." Furbies advertised for sale that didn't exist? Elvis Furbies and blue Furbies—the blue ones

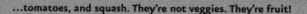

...tomatoes, and squash. They're not veggies. They're fruit!

were just regular white Furbies that had been dyed. "It's gotten so bad that people are almost taking dead rats and blow-drying them to fluff them up so they can sell them as Furbies," said a radio commentator.

Simon was telling the truth when she said there weren't any rare Furbies in 1998. That changed in 1999 with the FAO Schwarz Bejeweled Furby. The dazzling new Furby was decked out in a tiara, necklace, earrings, and bracelets made of gold, platinum, diamonds, rubies, and emeralds. Only five were made. Price tag on each: $100,000.

FURBY S.O.S. (SAVE OUR STATES)

Believe it or not, the National Security Agency (the NSA) had Furby on its radar. Because Furbies mimicked sounds that sounded as if they were "talking back" by recording what had been said, in 1999 they were banned from many federal buildings. Security officials worried that the toy could record classified information and repeat it. The NSA rulebook stated, "We are prohibited from introducing these items (recording devices, including Furbies) into NSA spaces." The toymaker's response: "The NSA did not do their homework. Furby is a clever toy, but it does not record or mimic voices. Furby is not a spy. " Apparently, the U.S. intelligence community did not receive that memo.

It takes 21.2 lbs. of whole milk (2.46 gallons) to make 1 pound of butter.

R.I.P. FURBY

After a few years of blinking and talking and trying (but failing) to learn English, even the most well-cared-for Furby can succumb to old age. The furry toy's eyes can get stuck half-open. It might start to make a mild buzzing noise. If hitting the reset button doesn't help, it's time to let Furby rest in peace or…in pieces. Furby owners whose furry friends have "died" may want to discover the "cause of death." There's a website for that: "Furby Autopsy." The site includes directions for how to skin a Furby as well as how to remove its ears and take apart its exoskeleton to see what "killed" it. Turns out Furby's guts are a collection of circuitry, motors, sensors, and a speaker. The site does warn that doing an autopsy on your Furby probably voids the warranty. Also, if Furby remains a beloved friend, don't do it. Furby's a lot like Humpty Dumpty. Once he's skinned, all the king's horses and all the king's men won't be able to put Furby together again.

*   *   *

FINE FEATHERED FUN

Q: Mum? Can I have a canary for Christmas?
A: No. You'll have turkey like everyone else.

Q: What's black and white, black and white, and black and white?
A: A penguin rolling down a hill.

Kid: How much is that duck?
Shopkeeper: Ten dollars.
Kid: Okay, could you please send me the bill?
Shopkeeper: Nope. You'll have to take the whole bird.

Q: What bird shows up every time you eat?
A: A swallow.

TOTALLY QUACKED ART

Beauty may be in the eye of the beholder but gross and disgusting? It simply is what it is.

BELLY-BUTTON-LINT BEARS

A hospital worker from Australia has been collecting his own belly-button lint in jars since 1984. Why? To make it into the *Guinness Book of World Records* for the largest collection of the stuff. But that's not the quackiest use of belly-button lint we've found. Rachel Betty Case uses belly-button lint to make tiny teddy bear sculptures. "Everyone thinks it's gross," says Case, "but bears are cute, and everyone can relate to a cute teddy bear." Cute? Some people find Case's work "disgusting." Case disagrees: "No way. I find eating meat and littering gross, but I'm faced with it every day. So what if my materials are a little in-your-face?"

DYEING FOR COLOR

"Mummy Brown" was popular with painters in the sixteenth and seventeenth centuries. But the warm brown color was made from pretty cold ingredients: ground-up human and cat mummies. French artist Martin Drölling reportedly used Mummy Brown made with the remains of French kings removed from tombs in the royal abbey of St-Denis in Paris. The Mummy Brown craze couldn't last. After all, there are only so many mummies available to grind into paint. According to Roberson's of London (an art paint company) in a 1964 *Time* magazine article: "We might have a few odd limbs lying around somewhere, but not enough to make any more paint. We sold our last complete mummy some years ago for, I think, £3 ($4.84). Perhaps we shouldn't have. We certainly can't get any more." How much paint does one mummy produce? In 1915 a London colourman (paint maker) reported that "one Egyptian mummy furnished sufficient material to satisfy the demands of his customers for twenty years."

MEAT ME AT THE MUSEUM

In 2008 at the Daneyal Mahmood Gallery in New York City, visitors weren't met by paintings or photographs. Instead, the stench of rotting meat greeted them like "a punch in the face." Every artwork on display was made of meat: sneakers made of meat, an American flag made of meat, and a cup and saucer made entirely out of bacon. Because none of the "art" on display was refrigerated, flies, maggots, and…the stench…became so overwhelming that the museum's neighbors threatened legal action.

*   *   *

QUACKED NEWS

LiveScience reports that your next hamburger might be grown in a lab rather than raised on the hoof. Scientists are experimenting with growing muscle tissue (meat) in petri dishes. Why? United Nations experts report that raising cattle for beef is "one of the most significant contributors to today's most serious environmental problems." Growing our burgers could change that.

...and drop to -243.4°F (-153°C) at night. *(Brrr...!)*

MOON MADNESS

Think moon phases are just for werewolves?

- Out of 59 types of nocturnal mammals studied by ecologists Laura Prugh and Christopher Golden, only one became more active beneath a full moon (the brightest moon phase): primates.

- When the moon is new (its darkest phase), coyotes howl as a group.

- European badgers pee more during a new moon.

- On a warm full moon each spring, the corals that make up Australia's Great Barrier Reef breed new coral when they all release their eggs and sperm at the same time. People say it looks like "drifting underwater snow."

- The moon's UV light makes scorpions glow in the dark. The brighter the moon, the brighter scorpions glow. They use the glow to tell them when they'd be easily spotted by predators. As the moon reaches fullness, scorpions seek shelter.

- Nocturnal animals often use visual signals to communicate at night. Eagle owls rely on white feathers just beneath their beaks to "talk" to other birds after dark. Under a full moon, eagle owls climb to higher perches where those flashy white feathers can be more easily spotted by their mates

- After studying 11,940 cases, researchers at the Colorado State University Veterinary Medical Center found that cats ended up in emergeny rooms 23 percent times more often during full moons. Dogs: 28 percent more often. Why? No one knows for sure, but maybe because it's bright enough to go out on the prowl.

The kangaroo rat can last longer without water than a camel can.

CLOUDY WITH A CHANCE OF...

Every day, all over Earth, there's a 100 percent chance of...
weather! And some of it's really weird.

A CHANCE OF...ICE METEORS

Most people have seen hail—those small pieces of ice that sometimes fall from storm clouds. But *megacryometeors*? Hopefully not. *Megacryometeors* are monster hailstones that can weigh up to several hundred pounds. And—we kid you not—these giant ice chunks usually plummet to the ground from a cloudless sky.

Reports of these "clear-sky ice-fall events" have been on the rise worldwide—more than 50 have been reported in the last seven years. Researchers have found evidence that the increase could be due to climate change. In 2007 a 20-pound megacryometeor crashed through the roof of an industrial warehouse east of Madrid, Spain, on a perfectly blue-sky day. In 2009 Chris Drab of Delta, British Columbia, heard a "thundering, whooshing noise." He looked up from mowing his lawn to see a monster chunk of ice falling from the (cloudless) sky. Within about 30 seconds, five more megacryometeors had fallen.

Jesus Martinez-Frias works at the Centre for Astrobiology in Madrid, Spain. He studies Tropospheric Global Warming.

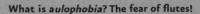

Martinez-Frias believes climate change on Earth's surface could be making the *tropopause*—the boundary in Earth's atmosphere between the troposphere and the stratosphere—"colder, moister, and more turbulent." That could create ideal conditions for ice crystals to grow much bigger than normal. (Climate change doubters: better wear a helmet, just in case.)

A CHANCE OF...SNOW ROLLERS

Snow rollers form layer upon layer like the snow balls you roll to make snowmen. They happen naturally when strong winds blow across flat, snow-covered areas. For snow rollers to form, three conditions have to occur: 1) the ground must be icy or be covered with a snow crust, 2) the layer of ice must be covered by wet, loose snow; and 3) winds must be strong and gusty. Unlike snow balls, snow rollers are somewhat cylindrical in shape, like rolled hay bales. Snow rollers can grow as large as two feet in diameter.

A CHANCE OF...MOONBOWS

Rainbows at night? Sounds crazy, but they do exist and they have a name: "moonbows." Moonbows are much rarer than rainbows. They're only seen when the moon is low and full. They're produced by light reflected off the surface of the moon (rather than from direct sunlight) refracting off of moisture in the air. And they are always in the opposite part of the sky from the moon. Compared to the average rainbow, moonbows are faint. Why? Because of the smaller amount of light reflected from the surface of the moon. However, moonbows can form at night near waterfalls, and those are usually easier to see. One of the best places to see moonbows: near the waterfalls in Yosemite National Park.

A CHANCE OF...A LIGHT SHOW

The Catatumbo River in Venezuela holds the title of "lightning capital of the world." More than 280 bolts per hour rip across the night sky on an average of 150 nights a year for 10 hours at a time. It happens so frequently that the phenomenon has become known as "Relampago de Catatumbo" (Catatumbo Lightning). It's also known as the Maracaibo Beacon and has acted as a natural "lighthouse" used for navigation by ships for ages.

Why the frequent lightning? The region has all the ingredients for a perfect storm—a combination of cold winds from the Andes Mountains and hot humid air rising from the marshlands below. Gasses from decomposing plants in the area may also contribute to the light show. They're believed to be the cause of the yellow, white, pink, and orange colors in the lightning.

A CHANCE OF...FISH

The picture book *Cloudy w ith a Chance of Meatballs* by Judi Barrett shows food falling from the sky onto the tiny town of Chewandswallow. Sound crazy? In Yoro, Honduras, hundreds of small silver fish rain from the sky onto the streets. According to locals, this has been happening since the 1800s. In the months of May or June, a large storm rolls through town, dumping a very heavy rainfall. Once the storm has passed, the streets flap and flop with live fish. The biggest mystery? The fish are not local species. Experts believe they may be coming from as far away as the Atlantic Ocean some 124 miles (200 km) away. One possible explanation: waterspouts over the ocean suck fish into the sky and then drop them over Honduras. A less exciting theory? The Yoro fish live in underground rivers and are being forced up onto the streets when excess rainfall floods those rivers.

South African Bernard Goosen scaled Kilimanjaro...in a wheelchair...twice!

HOLLYWOOD HOBBIES

These celebrities' hobbies just might surprise you.

CELEBRITY: Angelina Jolie
HOBBY: Collecting knives
THE STORY: The star started collecting knives at Renaissance fairs as a kid. Seems her mom had a passion for them, too. "My mom took me to buy my first daggers when I was eleven or twelve," she says. An old YouTube video shows Jolie demonstrating her knife-twirling skills to Conan O'Brien.

CELEBRITY: Johnny Depp
HOBBY: Collecting dolls
THE STORY: *The Pirates of the Caribbean* actor reportedly owns character dolls from his own movies, dolls based on cast members of *High School Musical*, and celebrity dolls such as Donny Osmond and Elvis. Rumor has it Depp accessorizes his dolls to reflect what's going on in show biz. One of the weirdest? A Lindsay Lohan doll, complete with ankle bracelet from her time under house arrest.

CELEBRITY: Claudia Schiffer
HOBBY: Spiders and Insects
THE STORY: The logo for Schiffer's fashion knitwear line feaures a doodle of a spider. "My inspiration is the forest and its dark side. It's not about the cute fox, more the fox eating its prey and 'pebbles' lying on the forest floor that could turn out to be spiders." The German model collects a variety of insects,

including mounted creepy-crawlies and insect paintings. "As a child, I was fascinated with spiders' webs sparkling with morning dew or just after the rain," says Schiffer.

CELEBRITY: Seth Myers
HOBBY: Collecting comics
THE STORY: Funny man Myers loves comic books. "I'm a proud reader and purchaser of comic books. I'm a long-time *X-Men* fan. I'd love to say I buy them for aging value, but I mostly buy them to read," he says. Not only does he read them, but he's written a comic book with fellow *Saturday Night Live* cast member Bill Hader, titled *Spider Man: The Short Halloween.*

CELEBRITY: Mila Kunis
HOBBY: Playing video games, being a Trekkie
THE STORY: Looks like Kunis has a geeky side—she's an avid *World of Warcraft* player. She also has a collection of vintage *Star Trek* figures and a photo signed by Leonard Nimoy. She's even attended a Trek conference in Las Vegas.

CELEBRITY: Paris Hilton
HOBBY: Frog hunting
THE STORY: The hotel heiress and reality TV star says she's against animal hunting, with one exception—frog hunting. She spends much of her spare time chasing the green guys. Where does the girl who has everything hunt? At her ranches in California and Nevada. Oh, and…on the island she owns. Hilton insists she's more humane than most hunters—she releases her prey back into the wild. The most frogs she's ever caught in one hunt? Ten.

Diseases carried by rats have killed more people than all the wars in human history.

QUACKY RITUALS

Sure...every religion has practices and traditions that seem a bit odd to outsiders. But these...well, you decide.

- The Church of Our Lord of the Good End in Salvador, Brazil, is said to have special powers to cure illness. Replicas of body parts made of wax or plastic—arms, legs, livers, hearts, lungs, eyes, and other miscellaneous body parts—hang from the walls and ceilings. They're brought here as an offering by those who come to pray for divine intervention to heal an injury or sickness—or to give thanks for a cure already attained.

- Cows aren't technically "sacred" in India. They're more like a protected species—but they do have historic ties with Hindu gods. Still, the reason Hindus don't eat beef is as practical as it is spiritual. Most rural Indian families have at least one dairy cow. The cow's milk nourishes the family's children.  Browned butter made from its milk is used for lamps. And the cow's dung supplies cooking fuel for the household. The cow also powers the plow when it comes time to plant the fields.

  There's even a "Cow Day"—Gopastami. On this holiday cows are washed and decorated in the temple and given offerings in the hope that they will continue to provide the gift of life to those who honor them.

- Sure, it sounds strange, but the ritual of praying for cars is practiced in many parts of the world, including the USA. Priests perform a blessing for safe driving by praying, chanting, sprinkling holy water, fanning perfumed smoke, drawing signs and symbols on vehicles, and decorating vehicles with flowers.

- In Thailand Buddhist priests bless new cars, motorbikes, and even new jet airplanes. In the Philippines, believers seek out Catholic priests to bless jeeps, cars, or motorcycles on Palm or Easter Sunday. Several states—including California, Rhode Island, and New Jersey—hold gatherings each year to bless motorcycles and their riders to keep them safe and accident-free.

- The Hindu religious holiday, Thaipusam, celebrates the birthday of one of their gods, Lord Murugan. Lord Murugan is said to have once killed an evil spirit named Soorapadman with a spear. In memory of that triumph, devotees use skewers, lances, large hooks, or a small spear called a *vel* to pierce parts of their bodies. Which parts? The most common practice is to use two skewers. One skewer is pushed *in* through the cheek just at the side of the mouth and then *out* through the other cheek on the other side of the mouth. The second skewer is pushed down through the tongue. This piercing is meant to show that the devotee has renounced the gift of speech to spend the holy day focused upon the deity. Does it hurt? Well…devotees say they go into "a spiritual and devotional trance " during which Lord Murugan keeps them from feeling any pain.

ANIMAL ODD COUPLES

In the wild, you don't need to tell animals to avoid predators.
It's instinctual. But under unusual circumstances?
Even natural enemies can become friends.

WHO: Themba & Albert
WHY: A deadly fall
WHAT HAPPENED: In 2008 tragedy struck South Africa's Sanbona Wildlife Reserve. A mama elephant fell off a cliff and died, leaving her six-month-old calf orphaned. When vets saw that no other elephant mothers in the herd would let Themba suckle, they rushed to save him, taking Themba to the Shamwari Wildlife Rehabilitation Center in the Eastern Cape.

At the time, Themba was still too traumatized to eat, so the staff introduced him to…Albert, a sheep from a nearby farm. At first Albert butted Themba's head and trotted to a shelter at the end of Themba's enclosure for the night. But by morning things had changed. Themba touched Albert on his woolly back as if "having a good sniff." Then he followed Albert into the fields, his trunk resting on Albert's spine as they searched for food. Fortunately for posterity's sake, a filmmaker captured the developing friendship on film.

When Themba and Albert weren't dozing together on a termite mound they'd devoured, the two chomped down on leaves from an acacia tree. That's perfectly normal for an elephant. But for a sheep? Not normal. Albert had watched Themba munching leaves, and then mimicked him. The Shamwari staff hoped Themba would grow strong enough to be reintroduced into the wild, but the calf died of colic two years after his rescue. His handlers and his best friend, Albert the sheep, were heartbroken.

WHO: A deer & Mother Goose

WHY: Loss of lifemate

WHAT HAPPENED: Who says fur and feather can't be friends? When a Canada goose lost her lifetime mate in 2011, she was left to fend for herself. At the time, she was nesting on six eggs in a giant urn in Buffalo, New York's Forest Lawn Cemetery. Somehow sensing the goose's situation, the resident white-tailed buck, who'd been living in the cemetery for years, stood guard near the goose and the urn for the entire period of gestation. While deer and geese are not known to help each other, the protective deer kept dogs and even park staff away by putting himself between the goose and the would-be intruders. The goslings hatched 21 days later, and mother goose ushered them onto the lawn. Their guardian buck headed for the hills to seek shelter but—as several crows soon learned—he kept a watchful eye on the goslings. Crows have been known to eat baby birds, and when the buck spotted crows near the goslings, he came back to chase them away.

*　　*　　*

ASK THE EXPERTS

You asked the questions: We found the answers!

Q: *Why don't frozen hot dogs cook in a microwave oven?*

A: "Frozen hot dogs do cook, but not very well. Pop one into a microwave oven and you will learn more about water and microwaves. One part of the hot dog will remain frozen while another part overheats and explodes open. The secret to exploding hot dogs is in the water, not in the microwave. Frozen water (better known as ice) locks the water molecules in a lattice structure, and the molecules just aren't as free to jiggle. The waves add energy, and a few start to break free from their chains. These free water molecules heat up rapidly while many frozen ones stay frozen. The free molecules eventually become so excited they blow a hole in the side of your hot dog. You end up with exploded hot dog goop only inches from a frozen part. To help solve this problem, microwave ovens usually have a defrost cycle for frozen food. The magnetron (the electron tube that produces the microwaves) turns off for short periods of time to allow heat from the thawed parts to melt more ice. Heat will then transfer to melt more ice before the magnetron kicks back into gear." (*How Do You Light a Fart? And 150 Essential Things Every Guy Should Know About Science* by Bobby Mercer)

It's all a blur! Experts believe that pigs' eyes can't focus.

ANSWER KEY

Page 15—**A SNAG RAM**

1. OLD MACDONALD
2. BET THE FARM
3. GET YOUR DUCKS IN A ROW
4. HOLD YOUR HORSES
5. FLEW THE COOP
6. COUNTING SHEEP
7. BORN IN A BARN

Page 18—**BRAWHK! QUIZ!**

1. b)
2. c)
3. b) There are about 370 known species.
4. c)
5. a) Parrots aren't native to North America, but thousands of birds have escaped homes and pet stores and now thrive in the wild.
6. b) Parrots eat seeds, fruit, nectar, nuts, and occasionally insects…but not other animals.
7. c)
8. a)
9. c) The Hyacinth Macaw has been known to reach a length of 39 inches and a weight of five pounds—bigger than a cat.
10. b)

Page 30–31—**WHO ORDERED FRIES?**

SOLUTION: First, we need to sort out the oldest and youngest kids, and figure out which two are twins.

Biddy is five years older than Diddy. It doesn't really matter how old they are, so let's say Biddy is 20. That makes Diddy 15. That would make Kiddy 18 (two years younger than Biddy). Piddy is also 18 (three years older than Diddy). So Kiddy and Piddy are twins.

The first and fourth orders listed on the receipt are from the twins, since they asked for no pickles. We can see that the twins—Kiddy and Piddy—both ordered fries.

The second order is the only one without a dessert, so that belongs to Biddy, who's the oldest. And he also ordered fries.

That means Diddy made the mistake and forgot to order fries. Maybe the others will share!

Page 63—**DUCK, DUCK...SILLY GOOSE!**
Garrett forgot about one duck. The two in Room I are the first and second ducks. The thirteenth duck is still waiting in the lobby.

Page 91—**BRAIN GAMES**
Two apples. Each pig will take one apple (half of what you have) and give the same apple back to you.

WHO DONE IT?
Owl, of course! Owls are nocturnal, which means they're usually out and about at night and asleep during the day. Sheep and Rooster are not nocturnal. They sleep at night and are up during the day. If all of the animals told the truth, then it wasn't Sheep and it wasn't Rooster—they both said they were innocent. Owl told the truth, but he never protested his innocence, so he's the guilty party.

Page 103—**BIRD BRAIN**

Countries	Birds
I. FRANCE	FINCH
2. BOTSWANA	BUDGERIGAR
3. CYPRUS	CONURE
4. ERITREA	ECLECTUS
5. KAZAKHSTAN	KAKARIKI
6. LATVIA	LORIKEET
7. MALTA	MYNAH

8. TUVALU	TURACO
9. RUSSIA	ROSELLA
10. SWEDEN	SISKIN
11. TOGO	TANAGER
12. QATAR	KEA
13. SERBIA	SERIN
14. RWANDA	RHEA
15. MONACO	MONAL
16. TAIWAN	WHYDAH
17. GRENADA	GRENADIER
18. CAMEROON	CURASSOW
19. LESOTHO	LEIOTHRIX
20. MICRONESIA	MESIA
21. SAMOA	SHAMA
22. CHILE	CHUKAR

Page 106—**WHERE'S ME?**

1. camera, 2. boomerang, 3. comedy, 4. meteor, 5. flame, 6. oatmeal, 7. elements, 8. comet, 9. camel, 10. amethyst

Pages 126–127—**HONKY TONICS**

1. C; 2. B; 3. B; 4. A and C; 5. C; 6. C; **Bonus:** Lydia E. Pinham's Vegetable Compound and Beef, Iron, and Wine Tonic can still be purchased today.

Page 139—**SAY WHAT?**

1. OINK
2. COCK-A-DOODLE-DOO
3. BAA
4. EEYORE
5. RUFF
6. MOO
7. PI-PI-PI
8. CLUCK
9. NEIGH
10. QUACK
11. HONK
12. MEOW

Page 156— **I AIN'T AFRAID OF NO**

1. e; 2. b; 3. f; 4. g; 5. h; 6. i; 7. d; 8. a; 9. c.

Page 180—**BIRDLANDIA**

1. B. Byrdstown, Tennessee
2. H. Chicken, Alaska
3. D. Bird-in-Hand, Pennsylvania
4. F. Goose Pimple Junction, Virginia
5. E. Eagleville, Missouri
6. B. Pigeon Forge, Tennessee
7. A. Turkey Scratch, Arkansas
8. B. Parrotsville, Tennessee
9. G. Birdseye, Indiana
10. I. Parrot, Kentucky
11. C. Buzzard Roost, Mississippi

Pages 208–209—**TOTALLY TUBULAR QUIZ**

I. c., 2. b., 3. b., 4. a., 5. c., 6. c., 7. a., 8. b., 9. c., 10. a.,
II. c., 12. a. How do your parents score on the **Rent-O-Meter?**

I–6 correct answers: Your folks were as lame (uncool) as you always thought. 7–I2 correct answers: Shocker of the new millenium! Your parents were totally tubular (very cool and probably even popular).

Page 217—**BIRD WORDS**

I. duck's	7. bird	I3. birds
2. quack	8. birds	I4. bird
3. bird (or eagle)	9. ducks	I5. chicken
4. dander	I0. pigeon	I6. nest
5. birds, feather	II. bird	I7. goose
6. egg	I2. bat	

THE
LAST PAGE

FELLOW BATHROOM READERS:

Bathroom reading should never be taken loosely—we must sit firmly for what we believe in, even while the rest of the world is taking pot shots at us.

Sit Down and Be Counted! Join the Bathroom Readers' Institute. It's free! Send a self-addressed, stamped envelope to: BRI, P.O. Box 1117, Ashland, Oregon 97520. Or contact us through our website at *www.bathroomreader.com.* You'll receive a free membership card, our BRI newsletter (sent out via e-mail), discounts when ordering directly through the BRI, and you'll earn a permanent spot on the BRI honor roll!

UNCLE JOHN'S NEXT *BATHROOM READER FOR KIDS ONLY* IS IN THE WORKS!

Don't fret—there's more good reading on the way.

Is there a subject you'd like to see us research? Write to us or contact us through our website and let us know. We aim to please.

Well, we're out of space, and when you've got to go, you've got to go. Hope to hear from you soon. Meanwhile, remember:

Go with the Flow!